THREE IN NORWAY

THREE IN NORWAY

BY TWO OF THEM

ILLUSTRATIONS BY THE AUTHORS

ASCHEHOUG

First published 1882
First Tanum-Norli edition 1968
Fifth printing 1995
ISBN 82-03-22125-4
Nor-Media a.s. - Oslo

PREFACE

"Three in Norway" is a classic. It was first published in England in 1882, in the glorious era when the savage country of Norway was being discovered by English adventure-seekers with fishing-rod in one hand, rifle in the other and their courage in both.

Apart from writing a brilliant and amusing book the "two of them", J. A. Lees and W. J. Clutterbuck made many shrewd observations on Norway and the natives. "Three in Norway" can certainly be read with the same pleasure today as when it first appeared, and the mountains, lakes and glaciers where the three friends found so much fun and enjoyment are still there. The book was reprinted several times, but the English edition has now been out of print for several years, and the Norwegian translation has been of little use to the readers the book was intended for: English-speaking visitors to Norway, past, present and future.

In making "Three in Norway" available in English once more we have preferred to maintain the original spelling – and misspelling – of geographical names, as we consider this part of the pioneer flavour.

CONTENTS

Introduction

HISTORY.

Our party consisted of three men, who shall be briefly described here. First 'the Skipper,' so called from his varied experience by land and sea in all parts of the world, but especially in Norway, whither we were now intending to go in search of trout, reindeer, and the picturesque. The Skipper is lank and thin, looking as though he had outgrown his strength in boyhood, and never summoned up pluck enough to recover it again. His high cheek-bones and troubled expression give one the idea of a man who cannot convince himself that life is a success, which is perhaps pretty nearly the view he actually takes of existence.

Secondly, 'Esau,' who received this name in consequence of the many points in which his character and history resemble that of the patriarch who first rejoiced in it: for our Esau, like his prototype, is 'a cunning hunter and man of the fjeld;' and we are sure that if he ever had such a thing as a birthright, he would willingly have sold it for a mess of pottage. Esau is short and joyous, and is one of those people who never indigest anything, but always look and always are in perfect health and spirits. It is annoying to see a man eat things that his fellow-creatures cannot without suffering for it afterwards, but Esau invariable does this at dinner, and comes down to

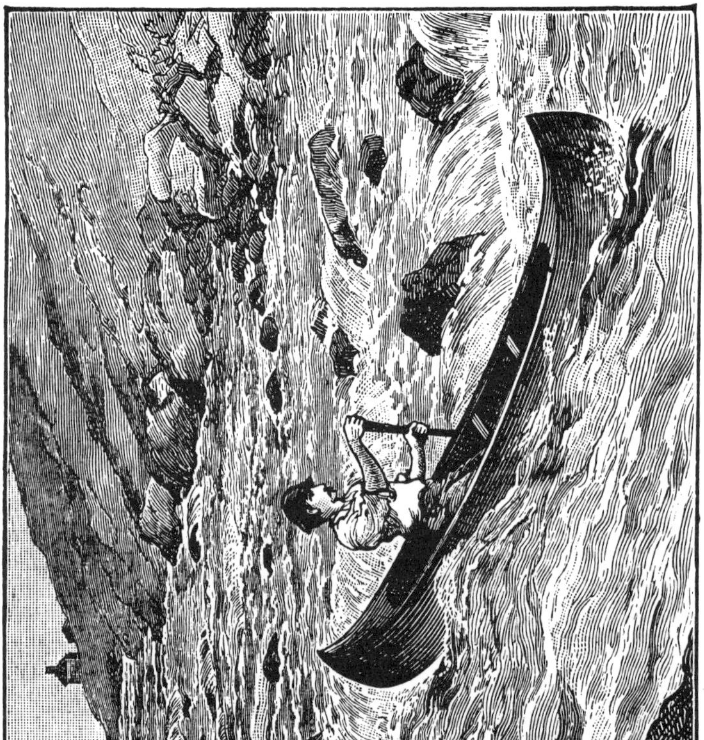

breakfast next morning with a provoking colour on his cheek and a hearty appetite. His office in this expedition was that of Paymaster; not because he possessed any qualifications for the post, but because the Skipper had conclusively proved that such employment was too gross and mundane for *his* ethereal soul, by constantly leaving the purse which contained our united worldly wealth on any spot where he chanced to rest himself, when he and Esau went to spy out the land two years before this.

Lastly, 'John,' so called for no better reason than the fact that he had been christened Charles: he had never yet visited the wilds of Scandinavia. John is an Irishman, whose motto in life is 'dum vivimus vivamus:' he is tall and straight, with a colossal light moustache. He generally wears his hat slightly tilted forward over his forehead when engaged in conversation; and the set of his clothes and whole deportment convey an idea that he is longing to tell you the most amusing story in the world in confidence. He is no gossip, and the anecdotes of his countrymen, of which he has an inexhaustible supply always ready, are merely imparted to his listeners from philanthropic motives, and because he longs for others to share in the enjoyment which he gleans from their mental dissection.

The general idea of the campaign was that the Skipper and Esau should leave England in the early part of July; fish their way up a string of lakes into the Jotunfjeld, getting there in time for the commencement of the reindeer season; establish a camp somewhere; and then that John, starting a month later, should join, and the three of us sojourn in that land until we were tired thereof. How we accomplished this meritorious design we have tried to relate in the following pages.

GEOGRAPHY.

The map of Norway, apart from Sweden, presents an outline something like a tadpole with a crooked irregular tail. The Jotunfjeld is an extensive range of the highest mountains which are to be found in Northern Europe: before 1820 A.D. they were totally unexplored, and at the present time they are still perfectly wild and desolate, their summits covered with eternal ice and snow, and even their valleys uninhabited. That part of the Jotunfjeld which we intended to make our goal and headquarters is situated about the middle of the tadpole's body, and nearly equidistant from Trondhjem and Christiania.

LANGUAGES.

It is customary when writing a book on any foreign country to scatter broadcast in your descriptions words and phrases in the language of that country, in order to show that you really have been there. We propose to depart from this usage in the course of this work; but if at any time the exigencies of narrative seem to demand the use of the foreign tongue, we have little doubt that the English language will provide an equivalent, which shall be inserted for the benefit of the uninitiated.

MATHEMATICS.

Foreigners have a curious prejudice which leads them to adopt different systems of coinage and measurement from those in favour in England. But shall a Briton pander to this prejudice by making any use of their ridiculous figures? Decidedly not. What matters it to us that a Norwegian land-mile contains seven of our miles, and a sea-mile four? We speak only of the British mile. What care we that the Norwegian krone is worth about 13½*d.?* Shall that prevent us from always calling it a shilling? Never! And shall the fact that it is divided into 10-øre pieces (which are little nickel coins worth about five farthings each) restrain us from alluding to them as the 'threepenny bits' which they so much resemble? Not while life remains.

EXTRA SUBJECTS.

Some of the statements that will be found in these pages may strike the reader as being, to say the least of it, improbable. We therefore wish to explain that all the incidents of sport and travel are simple facts, but that here and there is introduced some slight fiction which is too obviously exaggerated to require any comment.

CHAPTER I.

THE VOYAGE.

July 8.—At ten P.M. on the platform of the Hull station might have been seen the disconsolate form of Esau, who had arrived there a few minutes before. To him entered suddenly an express train, with that haste which seems to be inseparable from the movements of express trains, adorned as to the roof of one of its carriages by a Canadian canoe. From that carriage emerged the lanky body of the Skipper, and general joy ensued.

Then in the hotel the Skipper related his perilous adventures; how he had crossed London in a fourwheeler with the canoe on the quarter-deck, and himself surrounded by rods, guns, rugs, tents, and ground-sheets in the hold, amid the shouts of 'boat ahoy!' from the volatile populace, and jeers from all the cabs that they met (there are many cabs in London); how the station-master at King's Cross—may his shadow never be less! — had personally superintended the packing of the canoe on a low carriage which he put on to the train specially; and how the G. W. charged four times as much as the G. N. He had seen John the day before, and on being asked to 'wander about, and get some things with him,' the Skipper had replied that it was quite impossible, as his time was occupied for the whole day: but when John said, 'I wanted your advice chiefly about flies, and a new rod that I am thinking of buying,' he replied, 'Sir, I have nothing of the slightest importance to do; my time is yours; name the moment and place of meeting, and I will be there.' Then they twain had spent a happy day; for decidedly the next best thing to using your own rod is buying one for another man—at his expense.

Poor Esau had no charming experiences to relate; he was a little depressed because an intelligent tyke at Doncaster had looked into the horse-box in which his canoe was travelling, hoping no doubt to see some high-mettled racer, and had asked if 'yon thing were some new make o' a coffin.'

July 9.—At six o'clock we were safely aboard the good ship 'Angelo,' and saw our baggage stowed. It consisted of three huge boxes of provisions, weighing more than 100 lbs. each, two portmanteaus, two smaller bags, a tent, a large waggon-sheet intended to form another tent, a bundle of rugs and blankets, a large can containing all cooking utensils, four guncases, seven rods, a bundle of axes, a spade and other necessary tools, and the canoes with small wheels for road transport. Those wheels were the only things in the whole outfit that turned out to be not absolutely necessary. We did use them, but only once, and might have managed without them.

When the aforesaid was all on board, there did not appear to be much room for anything else in the steamship 'Angelo,' registering 1300 tons; yet this vast pile was destined to travel many miles over a desperately rough country in the two little canoes.

We were warped out of dock about eight o'clock, and steamed down the Humber with a west wind and a smooth sea. It was showery up to the moment of our departure, but as Hull faded from our sight it became fine, and with the shores of England we seemed to leave the cloud and rain behind.

July 10.—The day passed as days at sea do when the weather is all that can be wished, and the treacherous ocean calmly sleeps. The passengers were as sociable as any collection of English people ever are, and we spent the time very pleasantly chatting, smoking, eating enormously, and playing the ordinary sea games of quoits and horse-billiards.

CHAPTER II.

CHRISTIANIA.

Sunday, July 11.—We arrived at Christiania about nine at night, after a first-rate passage.

The Fjord was not looking as beautiful as usual, as there had been a great deal of rain, and the stormclouds and mist were still hovering about the low hills, so that no glories of the northern sunset were visible.

We arranged that the Skipper should go straight to the Victoria Hotel for rooms, as we heard that the town was very full, and Esau was to follow with the luggage. Now there was a young Englishman on board, very talkative, extremely sociable, remarkably kind-hearted, and overflowing with the best advice. He had gone round the whole ship entreating every one to go to the 'Grand.' as he intended to do, because it was by far the best hotel.

Just as the Skipper had engaged our rooms at the 'Victoria,' in rushed this guileless child of Nature, panting from the speed at which he had come from the quay, and the Skipper had the gratification of witnessing his discomfiture and listening to his apologies for having lied unto us, which of course he had done in order to get rooms for his own party at the 'Victoria.'

We say nothing against the 'Grand,' because we know it not, but any one who has once tried the 'Victoria' will go there again: the man who is not at home and happy there must be a very young traveller.

This hotel possesses a spacious courtyard, surrounded by galleries from which bedrooms and passages open, very much like that historical hostelry in the Borough at which Mr. Pickwick first encountered Sam Weller.

These galleries, and indeed most portions of the hotel, are made of wood, and the building is not of recent date, for now no houses in Christiania are allowed to be constructed of timber only.

In the centre of the court is a fountain which keeps up a gentle plashing, very pleasant to listen to on a day when the thermometer is at 90° in the shade, as it generally is about this time of year in Christiania. All round the fountain are small tables and chairs, ready for the little groups who will assemble at them after dinner for the cup of coffee and glass of cognac which form an indispensable part of a Norwegian dinner. The dinner itself is, during the summer months, always served in a large oblong tent in the same courtyard at 2.30, and a very pleasant meal it is, if you are not too much wedded to English habits to be able to secure an appetite at that hour. At short intervals down the table large blocks of ice are placed, which perform excellent service in helping to keep the tent cool.

Then there is another delightful resort, the smoking-room, which is upstairs on an extension of the gallery overlooking the courtyard. It also is covered by a sort of tent, in the roof of which divers strange and gruesome birds and beasts disport themselves, or seem to do so: we have reason to believe that they are stuffed, as we notice that the flying capercailzie never seems to 'get any forrader;' the fox stealing with cautious tread upon the timid hare unaccountable delays his final spring, but perhaps he is right not to hurry, for the hare does not appear to be taking any measures for her safety, but sits calmly nibbling the deeply dyed moss which it were vain to inform her is not good to eat. But there are other birds which we *know* are stuffed, for we helped to stuff them, and these are the sparrows, which come gaily flying in at the open side of the smoking balcony; hopping on the chairs and tables, pecking at the crumbs on your plate, and behaving generally in that peculiarly insolent manner which can only be acquired, even by a sparrow, after years of study, and the most complete familiarity with the subject. These birds are a source of endless delight to Esau, who certainly gives them more than can be good for them; they eat twice as much as the capercailzies, though the latter are considerably larger. And if the sparrows are not enough entertainment, there are tanks of gold-fish and trees of unknown species in pots; but neither of these perform very interesting feats.

In this room it is the custom of the ordinary traveller to have his breakfast and supper. Breakfast is very much like a good English one, except the coffee, which is not at all like English coffee, being perfectly delicious; but the supper is a meal peculiar to Norway, and is generally constructed more or less on the following principles:—

Caviare, with a fresh lemon cut up on it.

Norwegian sardines, garnished with parsley and bay leaves.

Cray-fish boiled in salt water.

Prawns of appalling magnitude.

Bologna sausage in slices.

Chickens.

Slices of beef, tongue, and corned beef.

Reindeer tongue.

Brod Lax (spelling not guaranteed), meaning raw salmon smoked and cut in thin slices.

Baked potatoes.

Good butter, and rolls which no man can resist, so fresh are they, and light, and crisp.

Drink: 'salon øl,' which is the best Norwegian beer.

This supper does not come in in courses, but the whole of it is placed on the table at once; not spread out all over the surface of the board as at home, but arranged in small oval dishes all round the consumer, and radiating within easy reach from his plate, making his watch-chain the centre of a semicircle, and thus entirely dispensing with that creaking-booted fidget the waiter. Such an arrangement cannot fail to coax the most delicate appetite. There is no coarse *pièce de résistance*; no vast joint to disgust you; but, like the bee, you flit from dish to dish, toying, now with a prawn, now with a

merry-thought, till you suddenly discover that you are unconsciously replete, and you rise from the table feeling that it was a good supper, and that existence is not such a struggle after all.

July 12.—We took our canoes to the railway station, and despatched them to Lillehammer this afternoon; they had been a source of great interest to all beholders since our arrival, especially to the Norwegians, who have all a sort of natural affinity with any kind of boat, and seemed very much pleased with the combined lightness and strength of their build. As far as we can learn, they are the first of the kind that have yet been brought to this country.

At the station they were surrounded by a crowd of inquiring Norsemen, all of them wondering much what the name of 'Nettie' on the bows of the Skipper's craft could mean, and spelling it over very slowly and carefully aloud. When we came away, one of them, evidently a linguist, had just translated it into his own language, and was proceeding to conjugate it as an irregular verb.

CHAPTER III.

BY RAIL AND LAKE

July 13.—We got our baggage safely booked, and ourselves also, after a scene of riot that was nothing like a football match, but something like Donnybrook Fair, and at last found ourselves in a compartment with five other passengers, all of whom had a most inconsiderate amount of luggage with them in the carriage, while we contented ourselves with four guns, seven fishing-rods, two axes, one spade, four hundred and fifty cartridges, two fishing-bags, and a pair of glasses. We calculated that we saved at least one and fourpence by taking these things with us; and although our fellow-passengers were rather profane at first they soon settled down, and we had time to digest the fact that we were one and fourpence to the good. It was very warm in there; outside the thermometer was 92° in the shade; but we survived it, and after that no mere heat has any terrors for us.

Two of our fellow-passengers were an Englishman and his wife, who had a maid travelling with them through to Trondhjem; and when getting the tickets the booking clerk informed them that there were no second-class through tickets issued, 'but,' he added 'this will do as well,' and handed them one first and one third through ticket, which we thought an extremely ingenious way out of the difficulty.

A railway journey is not interesting anywhere, and less so in Norway than other countries, as there is not even the sensation of speed to divert your mind, and keep you excited in momentary expectation of a smash. Uphill the pace is slow because it cannot be fast; downhill it is slow for fear of the train running away.

There are only two trains a day, one very early, one rather late, but timed to arrive at its destination before dark, for there is no travelling by night. Directly darkness comes on the train is stopped, and the passengers turned out into an hotel, where they remain to rest till dawn. From Christiania to Eidsvold is about a three-hour journey, and during that time the guard came to look at our tickets 425 times. He wanted to incite us to commit a breach of the peace, or to catch us offending against some of his bye-laws, and was always appearing at a new place; first at one door, then the other, anon peeping at us through the hole for the lamp, and again blinking from the next carriage through the ice-water vessel. But we were aware of his intention, and did nothing to annoy him, and always showed the same tickets till they were worn out, and then we produced strawberry-jam labels, which seemed to be quite satisfactory.

We reached Eidsvold at twelve, and went aboard the steamer 'Skibladner[1]),' where we found the canoes already nicely placed, lashed on the paddle-boxes.

We had a delightful voyage up the Mjøsen, on the most beautiful of Norwegian summer days, in the best of Norwegian steamers. The Mjøsen is the largest Norwegian lake,

[1]) The 'Skibladner' was built in 1856 and is certainly one of the oldest steamships in the world still in use. After a short rest on the bottom of the lake, this 'white swan of the Mjøsa' is now (1968) getting a face-lifting before being put back into service.

about fifty-five miles long, and the guide-books say it is 1440 feet deep, but we had not time to measure it, as we were busy admiring the scenery on the saloon table most of the way. This steaming up the Mjøsen is a very pleasant way of spending a fine day: the shores are nowhere strikingly beautiful, but always pretty and charming; the steamer goes fast, so that there is a sensation of getting on and not losing time. There are intervals of mild excitement whenever we come to a village, and take up or disembark passengers; generally speaking they come out in boats, but occasionally we come to a larger and more important place where there is a pier, or even a railway, and at these the excitement is greater and the crowd quite worthy of the name. The folks all take off their hats directly we get within sight, and continue to do so till they fade away or sink below the horizon; and we in the steamer all do the same. But the great attraction is undoubtedly dinner, which is uncommonly well served in the saloon, every luxury that can be obtained being placed before us, concluding with wild strawberries and cream of the frothiest and most captivating appearance.

We arrived at Lillehammer, about eight o'clock, and went to the Victoria Hotel, from the flat roof of which, after an excellent dinner, we enjoyed a pipe and one of the prettiest views, in a quiet homely style of prettiness, that any one could wish to see; just at our feet the wooden village, with its many-coloured houses and their red roofs; then some green slopes, and 100 feet below the vast extent of the Mjøsen lying calm and still and looking very green and deep, with the landing-stage and deserted steamers apparently quite close below us. On the opposite side of the lake highish hills covered with fir-trees, and to the right the river Laagen with its green waters hurrying down from the mountains in a broad and rapid stream as far as the eye could reach. Just across the road in front of the hotel there is a nice little stream which turns a saw, and rejoices in a cool splashing waterfall, the soothing sound of which refreshes us by day and night. The same torrent can be seen higher up the mountain in a place where it makes some rather fine falls, which only look like a long white rag fluttering amongst the trees at this distance. This was the view we had at midnight, when it was, apparently, no darker than immediately after sunset, and a good deal lighter than it generally is in London at midday; the while the sky was covered with the rich glow of colouring which can only be seen in the Northern summer.

There were two Englishmen with us on the roof, with whom, aided by coffee, we roamed over the greater part of the civilised and uncivilised world—Australia, Canada, Japan. Turkey, and Ceylon, and we all agreed that none of them can 'go one better' than a summer night in Norway.

CHAPTER IV.

BY ROAD

July 14.—We arose pretty early, wishing to get over thirty-eight miles of ground before evening, which with the canoes would be a long day's work; as we had the natives to contend with, who by reason of their dreadfully lazy habits are most difficult to 'bring to the scratch.'

We have decided, after long experience, that nothing that you can do has any effect in hurrying them; but that it is quite possible to make them slower by losing your temper, or taking any vigorous measures of acceleration. They seem to get more deliberate and aggravatingly slow as they grow older.

Norwegian boys are distractingly restless and full of energy, and look as if they have had nothing to eat, which is generally the actual fact, judging by an English standard of what constitutes food. At the age of fifteen they become better fed, and their energy departs altogether, and after entirely disappearing it keeps getting less every year. A full-grown man does not seem to need much food, certainly not as much as an Englishman, and prefers that of the worst kind, conveyed to the mouth at the end of a knifeblade. We have never noticed any description of food which he does not make sour, rather than eat it when sweet. Bread, milk, cream, and cheese, jam and cabbages, for instance, are articles which he prefers fermented or sour. He reminds one of the Cockney who complained that the country eggs had no flavour, or of the Scotchman who, replying to the apologies of a friend in whose house he happened to get a bad egg, said, 'Ma dear freend, ah *prefair* 'm rotten.'

But his laziness and love of nasty food are almost the only bad qualities that we have discovered in him. He is ridiculously honest,[1] and his kindness and hospitality are beyond praise. This morning, however, the laziness was the quality chiefly conspicuous, and though we ordered our conveyances last night and got up early (for us), we did not succeed in starting till twelve o'clock.

We first despatched the canoes and baggage packed on a kind of low waggon, and then got into a double cariole (which is something like a gig) ourselves, and drove gaily off along

[1] Save, perhaps, on three points–fishing tackle, strong drinks, and straps or pieces of cord; which may be commited to memory as 'a fly, a flask, and a fastener.'

the Trondhjem road. We did not, however, follow it far, but turning to the left down a steep hill, we crossed the Laagen by a long and rather handsome bridge, and then up a winding road on the further side, all looking very pretty on such a glorious day. The road became more picturesque the further we got from Lillehammer, every turn bringing us to some fresh combination of mountain, pine-trees, rock, and waterfall—especially rock. There are so many tracts of country in Norway entirely composed of rock, that, as Esau remarked, 'probably no one will ever find a use for it all.'

We lunched at a nice little station called 'Neisteen;' a delicious meal off trout, strawberries and cream, and fladbrod, for which they charged us a shilling each.

'Fladbrod' is the staple food of the country folk in Norway; they make it of barley-meal, rye-meal, or pea-meal, but the best and commonest is that composed of barley-meal. It is simply meal and water baked on a large, flat, circular iron, and is about the thickness of cardboard, of a brownish colour, and very crisp. The taste for it is easily acquired in the absence of other food, and with butter it becomes quite delicious—to a *very* hungry man.

About a mile from our journey's end we were overtaken by a Norwegian student on a walking tour, who spoke a little English and walked with us the rest of the way, as he too was bound for Dalbakken.

We reached it at midnight, and were not much gratified to find that it was a very small poor building, and that our luggage had not arrived. We had been hoping against hope that it might have done so, as we had not seen it anywhere on the road. The next pleasant discovery was that four other travellers had arrived before us and taken all the rooms. This fact was first conveyed to our minds by seeing four pairs

of socks hanging out of the upstair windows to dry; at which sight we began to suspect that things were going to turn out unpleasant for us; but at last we got a room with one very small bed between us. We tossed for this bed, and the Skipper won; so Esau passed the night on the floor, on a sheepskin and was very comfortable—at least he said so next morning. The natives here were much impressed by all our habits and belongings, but especially by our sleeping with the window open; wherefore the old woman of the Sæter[1] below kept bouncing into the room at intervals during the night to see us perform that heroic feat; and though it was flattering to be made so much of, still fame has its drawbacks.

The general appearance of the place caused us to expect nightly visitations from other foes, not human, but to our surprise there were none.

Dalbakken is only three-quarters of a mile from a lake called Espedals Vand, where we propose to commence our cruise. It is beautifully situated on a small flat bit of ground halfway up the north side of the gorge: the hills on the south side not far away are so steep that they could not be climbed by all the branded alpenstocks that Switzerland ever produced. Looking to the east the gorge is very wild and grand, covered with pine-trees and steep crags, and no dwelling in sight; while to the west, in which direction Espedals Vand lies, it is more level and open, and slopes gradually downwards again, Dalbakken itself being the highest point in the track.

CHAPTER V.

THE FIRST CAMP.

July 15.—We slept well, and at eight o'clock the Skipper, always first to wake, got up, and looking out of the window saw thence the four bad men who had taken the rooms before us and hung their socks out of the window, just starting on

[1] A Sæter is a mountain farm, to which all the cattle are driven during the summer, so that the Lowland pastures can be mown for hay.

their journey, and looking as if they did so with an easy conscience.

Some men can carry with a light heart and gay demeanour a weight of crime that would wreck the happiness of less hardened ruffians.

Then he turned his gaze in the opposite direction, and oh, joy! our luggage and boats were in sight, and arrived directly afterwards. The man in charge said he had travelled all night with them without sleeping, and, to judge from his appearance, we imagined that his statement was correct. He had been sitting on the Skipper's bag for thirty-eight miles, and from the state of its interior we calculated his weight to be about twenty-two stone. He was very ill-tempered after his mere trifle of a journey and vigil, and asked for more money on hearing that he had three-quarters of a mile further to go. This was very sad, and we thought showed an unchristian spirit; but we sternly urged him forward, and all ended happily on our arrival at Espedals, when we paid him his money and a shilling extra.

It only took us a quarter of an hour to get to the lake, and after unpacking there and dismissing the men we put the canoes into the water, and then put water into the canoes until they sank; while we sat on the shore watching the trout rising all over the rippled surface of the lake, occasionally eyeing our sunken canoes in an impatient, longing sort of way, but never attempting to start on our great voyage.

These tacties to an inexperienced 'voyageur' might look like the acts of an ordinary lunatic; but it should be explained that the long exposure to the sun which the canoes had undergone had caused them to leak badly, and they required soaking to swell up the joints, before they could be intrusted with our valuable property and persons. Besides this we were hungry,

and thought it a good opportunity for lunch, and had to make some previously arranged alterations in the baggage with a view to lightening it. As long as the land journey lasted, strength was the chief object to aim at, but now lightness was of more importance. About one o'clock, when we had got all our things aboard and were just starting, a strong head-wind arose. This was always our luck. We decided to make only a short voyage. The waves were fairly big, but the canoes weathered them bravely, though they were very low in the water, and we had to keep the pumps going (*i.e.*, mop them out with our sponges) during the whole voyage.

We landed not more than a mile and a half from the end of the lake, and found a very nice camping-ground about ten yards from the shore on the south bank, with what the poets call 'a babbling brook' close to it; pitched the tent, and had

a simple dinner of bacon, eggs, and jam, the last dinner during our trip at which trout did not find a place. Then we sallied forth in the canoes to fish. Esau was the last to leave the shore, and as he paddled off he noticed the Skipper's rod in the familiar Norwegian shape of a bow, and found him struggling with two on at the same time, both of which he landed, and found to be over 1 lb. each. 'First blood claimed and allowed.' to quote the terse language of the prize ring. Not a bad beginning, but we only got a few more about the same weight. They came very short, but were remarkably game fish when hooked, and in first-rate condition. We turned in about eleven, when it began to rain a little, and slept with our heads

under the blankets, the mosquitoes being in countless multitudes.

July 16.—Any natives who see our camp when rowing past come to shore to inspect us and our belongings. They all adopt the same course of procedure. They land, and stare, and say nothing; then they pull up their boat and make it safe, and advancing close to the tent stare, and say nothing either to each other or us. Then Esau says confidentially, as if it was a new and brilliant idea (he has done exactly the same thing some scores of times), 'We'd better be civil to these fellows; perhaps they could bring us some eggs, and they look pretty friendly.' The natives are all the time staring and saying nothing. Then Esau remarks in Norwegian, 'It is fine weather to-day; have you any eggs?' To this the chief native replies at great length in his own barbarous jargon, and Esau not having understood a single syllable answers, 'Ja! ja! (yes), but have you any eggs?' Then aside to the Skipper, 'Wonder what the deuce the fool was talking about?' Soon the natives perceive that their words are wasted, and relapse into the silent staring condition again, and after a time and a half, or two times, they depart as they came. Sometimes they return again with eggs in a basket, when we pay them well and give them some fish; at other times they look upon us as dangerous lunatics, and avoid us like the plague.

The beach here was capital for bathing, and we enjoyed a delightful tub this morning, the more pleasant indeed because at Dalbakken we slept in our clothes, and only had a soap-dish to wash in next morning. Immediately after bathing we lit a fire, and the cook commenced operations; the office of cook being held alternately by each of us for one day. The man from Dalbakken brought us some milk, so we indulged in coffee. When we have only 'tin milk' we drink tea; for though tin milk will do fairly with tea, we think it wretched with coffee. After breakfast we each took our canoe, and went fishing wherever the spirit moved us, taking lunch with us. On a day of this sort, if the fish are rising, we have a great time, and if they won't rise we lie on the bank in the sun and smoke, or sketch, or kill mosquitoes, and have a great time in that case also, so that the hours pass in a blissful round of enjoyment, and all is peace. Having each one his own ship we are independent, only taking care to return to camp about six o'clock to get dinner ready. After that there is nearly always a rise, and we fish till about eleven, when we generally turn in, though it is by no means dark by that time; and on a few occasions, when the fish were rising very well, we have fished on all through the night and into the next day, losing count of the almanack, and conducting life on the principles of going to bed when tired, and eating when hungry, so that, like the Snark, we might be said to—

> 'Frequently breakfast at five o'clock tea,
> And dine on the following day.'

There was very little wind to-day, and these fish being very shy, and apt to come short, it was almost impossible to get them without a ripple until evening, when large white moths began to show on the water, and the trout became bolder; consequently we did not make great bags, though the fish caught were very good ones.

At night there was one of the most lovely sunsets ever seen. The sun went down right at the other end of the lake, so that we had an uninterrupted view, with all the glorious colours of the sky reflected in the water; and we agreed that the effects about half past ten this evening formed as good a symphony in purple and orange as a man could expect to find out of the Grosvenor Gallery.

July 17.—The morning began with a dead calm, but this soon gave place to such a wind down the lake that we were induced to strike the camp, pack the canoes, and proceed on our voyage into the unknown.

We started soon after eleven, lunched near Megrunden,[1] and saw there two black-throated divers on the lake, which Esau pursued for some time, but of course never got near them. Some of the dives they made to avoid his advancing canoe seemed to be about half a mile in length. Just below Bøle we caught several fish, but kept paddling on with our favourable wind, casting every now and then in likely places, and soon came to a rapid with a rough bridge thrown across its upper end. The rapid was very shallow, so that we did not dare to attempt tc run it with loaded boats, and had to make a portage. Even then we got a few bumps in running it, but arrived at the bottom all right. Now the scene changed; we were in a smaller and narrower part of the valley; buildings had entirely disappeared; there was nothing to be seen but gloomy pine forests and black-looking mountains; the weather also was quickly changing, and evidently intending to be wet and stormy; so we pushed on rapidly, one coasting on each side of the lake till we reached its further extremity, where Esau was nearly swamped crossing the waves, as the wind began to blow harder every minute. Soon the rain was upon us, while we looked for a camping-ground but found none, as the shores were everywhere very swampy for a quarter of a mile inland. At length we came to a second rapid, where the natives have thrown a clumsy weir across for some unknown purpose, and here we found a fairly dry spot, made our portage in heavy rain and wind, with a great deal of

[1] The various places mentioned on the voyage are not villages, as one might imagine from the dot that marks them on the Ordnance map, but generally only a single one-roomed log hut, and for the most part not inhabited or habitable.

groaning, misery, and brandy and water; pitched the tent, and after struggling for about half an hour, got a dyspeptic fire to fizzle, and so cooked some fish and eggs, and then had tea in the tent. After this we were a little more comfortable, as it was very nice and dry inside; but it was midnight before we had finished all our portage, got the canoes down into the next lake, and made everything snug for the night, so that we were quite exhausted, as our day had commenced at seven A.M. The mosquitos were more numerous here than at any place we have yet seen.

Sunday, July 18.—It rained all night, but, as Tweedledum said of his umbrella, 'not under here,' and a ditch we made last night kept our floor quite dry. Lighting a fire for breakfast was a toilsome business, but at last we found some wood dry enough to burn. It continued raining in a nice keep-at-it-all-day-if-you-like kind of manner, so we resided in the tent and read, and indulged in whisky and water for lunch to counteract any ill effects of the reading—for some of it was poetry.

CHAPTER VI.

MISERY.

July 19.—It rained all night again and all day. This was dreadful, and not at all like Norway.

We have always made a rule that we may fish on Sunday, but not shoot. Some people draw an even finer distinction, and say it is allowable to shoot with a rifle, but not with a gun; this we have always thought too subtle. Now yesterday was Sunday, and Esau having observed two divers on the lake

while the Skipper was out fishing, went and secreted himself with a gun where he expected them to come over, hoping that they would be alarmed by the other canoe on its return. This soon happened, and they flew within forty yards of him. Both barrels were discharged, and Esau returned to camp, muttering something about 'birds of that kind having immortal bodies if they hadn't immortal souls.' The result of Sabbath - breaking was no doubt this miserable weather.

July 20.—Still rain, and nothing but rain; it stopped for an hour or two last night, and the lake looked uncommonly pretty among its dark surroundings, but the downpour soon began again.

In our desperation yesterday afternoon we arranged with a native, whom the Skipper discovered, to bring a horse and sleigh to-day to meet us at the next rapid, and help us down with our baggage to Olstappen. Therefore we get up early and were down at the rapid about ten o'clock, where we found our man waiting. The rain at this period was the worst variety we have yet seen, and it has tried all kinds during the last four days. We packed everything on the sleigh, covered it with our ground-sheets, and then put the wheels on our canoes, and followed down the track.

There is a saw-mill halfway down the river which is simply perfect. It is perched on piles over the middle of the stream, where it dashes through a rift in a huge black cliff, and the water goes tearing past down a long shoot made of logs, and plunges down at the end churned into a mass of white foam, with noise and spray that quite bewilder one.

We got down to Olstappen at last, not without a good deal of hard work, and paid our man 4*s*. 6*d*. On our way we met a Norwegian tourist, who was on a walking tour with his sister, and had left her rained up, so to speak, in a Sæter, and was strolling about in the forest to wile away the time; he spoke a very little English, and we had a long talk with him; as he had a fellow-feeling for us, and was quite ready to curse the rain with us or any one else.

The Norwegians, men and women, seem to go a good deal on walking tours, and probably know infinitely more of their fatherland than does the average Briton of his island, the superiority of which he seldom fails to impress on the long-suffering foreigner.

July 21.—Hurrah! the rain stopped during the night, and this morning actually the sun shone out now and then. We heaped up a huge fire and dried all our belongings, and then had nearly a whole day before us free for fishing.

A voyaging day is a big business. We calculate that it takes us two and a half hours to pack up from an old camp, break-fast, and get aboard ship; but to pitch the camp in a new place takes much longer. First you have to find a suitable place, often a matter of great difficulty in a country like this, where level spaces a yard square are very rare; dig a trench; pitch the tent, and arrange everything in it; collect firewood, and make a place for the fire; see that the boats and everything about the tent are safe from harm should the stormy winds begin to blow; and then cook dinner. All this cannot be done under three hours of hard work; so that if in addition you propose getting over a considerable amount of ground, it is sure to be a long and toilsome day. But the following day you wake up with a glorious feeling of duty performed and pleasure to look forward to.

The Skipper, with a hankering after cleanliness, washed a lot of clothes, and himself, having left the rain to perform the latter operation for the last two or three days; but Esau, not being troubled with any such absurd remnants of civilisation went up the river reconnoitring in his natural condition. He came back to dinner in a perfectly rapturous state, having caught a remarkably nice bag of fish, got a beautiful view of the Jotunfjeld Mountains, and found a waterfall, which he said was the best in Norway, and therefore in the world. The Skipper had tried the lake in the afternoon without success, so after dinner we both went out and soon discovered the reason. Seven boats full of natives were out with a huge flue net, which they shot in a circle, and then beat the water enclosed till all the wretched fish were in the net. We saw them get thirty in one haul, and besides this there was a boat 'ottering;' and although we captured a few fish, it was obvious that with all this netting it would be impossible for the lake to be good.

CHAPTER VII.

HAPPINESS.

July 22.—This was a really fine day, such as we consider proper to Norway; no uncertain half-and-halfness, but a day when an untiring sun shone down from an immaculate sky; and everything looked lovely. Our tent was on a nice bit of turf close to the Vinstra River, which is about as broad as the Thames at Eton, but with probably twice the volume of water, and certainly three times its rapidity; it rushed past our door at such a pace that no boat could stem it; and as far as we could see up the reach it came down in an equally swift torrent, so that all day and all night there was a swilling, rushing sound very pleasant to hear, and creating a sensation of coolness in warm weather. Esau considered it just the *beau idéal* of a trout stream, for any fish hookd in it gave a lot of trouble before he was safe in the bag. It en intoa the lake about a quarter of a mile from our tent, forraing a good-sized delta at its mouth. At the further side of themdelt there was some fishermen's huts (from which emanated the seven boatloads of natives whom we saw yesterday netting), and thence a track leads up the banks of the river to a lake called Slangen, two miles away.

The inhabitants of these huts came in a boat this morning to see our camp while we were at breakfast inside the tent. They poked their heads in, grinning and staring, and saying nothing. Then we did the honours, showed them our most interesting possessions—American axes, fly books, knives, rods, &c., with all of which they were greatly impressed; then one picked up a bar of yellow soap that was lying on a box, and they all 'wondered much at that;' then we talked to them for a brief space, chiefly out of 'Bennett's Phrase Book,' and considered the interview at an end, but they *would* not go, and remained silently staring at all our movements. So at last we ignored their presence altogether, which we have found the most effectual way of getting rid of a Norwegian peasant, and they gradually departed one by one till only one was left. To this man we gave a cup of our now cold coffee, which was not at all good, especially when compared with the delicious coffee which is always forthcoming even in the meanest Norwegian hut. He drank this, for they consider it a breach of etiquette to refuse proffered food; and immediately left, as if he remembered an engagement, having first thanked us in a rather constrained manner.

We were glad when our callers were gone, for we had found them 'difficult,' as the French say; but we took advantage of their arrival to make arrangements with one of them to bring three ponies and sleighs to the other side of the delta to-morrow morning, when we hope to renew our journey.

After this we both went up the river on opposite sides; for the Skipper had become inflamed by a wish to see the waterfall which Esau discovered yesterday.

One of the great advantages of Norway consists in being able to leave your tent and all other belongings quite to themselves, even when you know that there are several people about, and shrewdly suspect that the place where you have made your camp is a hay meadow belonging to one of them. We had a dim idea that such was the case here, not because there was any grass, but because there were very few stones, and a Norwegian mows down everything for hay except the stones. The Skipper came back with a very pretty bag of fish; he had been up to the fall, and thought it quite deserved all Esau's commendation; and his opinion is worth more because he has seen many of the great American falls and other stock sights of the world. It is not marked on the Ordnance map; there is no path to it, or near it, but you come on it suddenly by following the river up through the pine forest, and on turning a corner see the whole body of the Vinstra shooting over a cliff in one mad leap of perhaps a little more than a hundred feet. Of course the height and volume of water are insignificant compared with many falls, but the beauty of its situation can scarcely be excelled; and to us its greatest charm is its solitude and freedom from paths, tourists, and all the other unpleasant attributes of show places.

We have probably been repaid for the miseries of the last week by the beauty of our waterfall, the volume of which has doubtless been much increased by the exceptional rain of the last few days.

Early to bed—

July 23.—And early to rise. We breakfasted soon after seven, and then packed everything, and crossed the mouth of the Vinstra in two Norse boats, assisted by two or three men who had come to help our horses and sleighs on the journey. We had terrible difficulty in getting the canoes placed in what we considered a safe position on the sleighs, but it was done at last, and the motley caravan started about 10.30.

First the noble owners; then a man who had got nothing on earth to do with the affair, then two women laughing and yelling like lunatics, then a sleigh drawn by a large pony, and carrying two boxes, cans, guns, and canoe; next some boys urging the large pony to herculean exertions; then the organiser of the transport department, who was apparently a professional fool, by the inordinate laughter which his every action caused; then some more women, and a smaller pony and sleigh, with the other canoe and all the rest of the luggage excepting one bag; lastly, another man leading an extremely small pony and sleigh with absolutely nothing on it, the man carrying the remaining bag for fear of tiring the pony. This mob of loafers had arrived in boats from Svatsum, which is a small village five miles distant at the north end of Olstappen. But they only accompanied us for a quarter of a mile, when they all departed except the three men, who remained to manage the ponies.

The pace was not very great, about a mile an hour, for these little ponies insisted on stopping to rest every hundred yards when the path was good, and every twenty when it was bad.

We followed the river till we crossed the Slangen bridge; after that the path began to rise and get rapidly worse. We strolled along very leisurely, sitting down from time to time to rest and admire the view. The scenery was occasionally very beautiful, with the Jotun Mountains gleaming white in the background; and the forest itself was an endless delight, with its hoary moss-covered pine-trees, and many-coloured carpet of berry-bearing plants, and the delicious odours with which a Norwegian forest in summer always abounds. In a fir-tree here Esau came upon a family of cole titmice, and another of creepers, all very busy swinging themselves about, and creeping up and down the tree in search of dinner. They appeared to take a certain amount of interest in his proceedings, but showed no fear, and after watching them a long time he put the point of his rod up to one of the titmice, which actually pecked it rather angrily, but seeing that it made no impression took no further notice, but returned to its occupation of collecting food. In the next tree was a little spotted woodpecker which they call a 'Gertrude bird.' The story is so prettily told in 'Forest Life in Norway and Sweden,' that it shall be inserted here.

'This woodpecker—or an ancestor of hers—was once a woman, and one day she was kneading bread in her trough, under the eaves of her house, when our Lord passed by leaning on St. Peter. She did not know it was our Lord and His apostle, for they looked like two poor men who were travelling past her cottage door. "Give us of your dough for the love of God," said the Lord. "We have come far across the fjeld, and have fasted long."

'Gertrude pinched off a small piece for them, but on rolling it in the trough to get it into shape, it grew, and grew, and filled up the trough completely. "No," said she, "that is more than you want;" so she pinched off a smaller piece and rolled it out as before, but the smaller piece filled up the trough just as the other had done, and Gertrude put it aside too, and pinched a smaller bit still. But the miracle was just the same, the smaller bit filled up the trough as full as the largest-sized kneading that she had ever put into it.

'Gertrude's heart was hardened still more; she put that aside too, resolving as soon as the strangers left her to divide all her dough into little bits and to roll it out into great loaves. "I cannot give you any to-day" said she. "Go on your journey; the Lord prosper you, but you must not stop at my house."

'Then the Lord Christ was angry, and her eyes were opened, and she saw whom she had forbidden to come into the house, and she fell down on her knees. But the Lord said, "I gave you plenty, but that hardened your heart, so plenty was not a blessing to you. I will try you now with the blessing of poverty; you shall from henceforth seek your food day by day, and always between the wood and the bark" (alluding to the custom of mixing the inner rind of the birch with their rye-meal in times of scarcity). "But forasmuch as I see your penitence is sincere, this shall not be for ever; as soon as your back is entirely clothed with mourning this shall cease, for by that time you will have learnt to use your gifts rightly."

'Gertrude flew from the presence of the Lord, for she was already a bird, but her feathers were even now blackened from her mourning, and from that time forward she and her descendants have all the year round sought their food between the wood and the bark; but the feathers of their back and wings get more mottled with black as they grow older, and when the white is quite covered the Lord takes them for His own again.

'No Norwegian will ever hurt a Gertrude bird, for she is always under the Lord's protection, though He is punishing her for the time.'

Whether this is the true reason or not, the fact remains that the bird is never harmed by any one, and is as tame as possible.

We continued climbing slowly up the hill till about one o'clock, when we came out above the forest on an open plateau covered with rocks, grass, and low scrub: this was the Fjeld. At Finbøle Sæter we stopped to refresh on milk. The road—which had gradually dwindled from a decent path to a sleigh track, then a footpath, a cow-path, and a goat-path, just sufficient to swear by, or at—now lost itself altogether. The men had been complaining that it was a 'dole vei' (bad road) soon after the start, now they said it was 'schlamm' —a very expressive word; and Esau agreed with them, and said it was 'damm schlamm,' which does not sound like proper Norsk; but it was such heartrending work to see our beloved canoes bumping and jolting along, every moment in imminent danger of getting staved in, that to indulge in a few such

Norwegian idioms was only human; and we decided to walk on and spare ourselves the agony of the sight; so, taking the bearings of 'Fly Sæter'—which was our destination for the evening—we rambled on across the fjeld—a splendid walk, with some of the most beautiful mountains in Norway all round us.

We got on very well with the assistance of an Ordnance map and compass, till we came to the river Hinøgle, after passing Hinøglid Sæter. The bridge here was not in the place marked on the map, so that after crossing it we had some trouble in finding Fly Sæter, and might perhaps have perished miserable like the Babes in the Wood, had we not opportunely met a mediæval fisherman in a red night-cap, looking like one of the demons in 'Rip van Winkle,' who was going thither and conducted us. We arrived at seven o'clock, and appeased our hunger with the usual meal of trout and coffee, and *such* cream!

The sæter was a long low house, with three little rooms and only two windows. Its legitimate tenants were a very nice man and his equally nice wife and three children; but there were some occasional visitors here to-night in the shape of ourselves, our three men, the mediæval angler, and another traveller, twelve altogether to be apportioned among four beds; and to make matters worse, the rooms were continually invaded by sheep, pigs, and goats, of which there were a large stock.

The Norwegians are so uniformly kind to all their animals, that their tameness is really troublesome; they insist on going where they like, and following one about begging for food like dogs, causing the Skipper to exclaim,—

'Ite domum saturæ, venit Hesperus, ite capellæ;' which he translated—

'Out of the house in the evening! Get out, ye goats of the sæter!'

We slept in the cheese-room very comfortably, one on the floor, the other one on a good hay bed, and were warm for the first time for several nights, as we have not had sufficient blankets in the tent. Where the other ten people slept we did not inquire, but hoped they were happy. Our men and sleighs did not arrive till 10 P.M., at which time a most glorious sunset was going on, so that we could not attend to them at once. The sky, at first blue and yellow, gradually deepened into purple and orange, and finally the most brilliant red and almost black clouds, the hills all the time glowing with exquisite tints. After it was concluded we turned to the men, and were much delighted to find that nothing was smashed so far; the men had been very careful, and took eleven hours to perform a journey of ten miles.

CHAPTER VIII.

FLY SÆTER.

July 24.—The morning was again beautifully fine, and the coffee at the sæter was passing delicious, even for this country, where coffee is always good. No doubt the chief reason of this is that it is never roasted and ground till just when it is wanted, not only at the hotels, but at the smallest sæters. The grinding of coffee and the frying of trout are grateful sounds to the wearied traveller, and if the walk across the fjeld has failed to give him an appetite, he has still the chance of obtaining one from the fragrant aroma of the roasting berry.

This sæter is in a most beautiful situation, perched on a little flat bit of ground on the mountain side, and looking down on a wide-stretching sea of grey undulating hills, with lakes lying among them dotted about near and far, and all the lower ground covered with the everlasting pine forest. To the south can be seen the river Hinøgle, which runs out of the Heimdal Lakes, threading its way with gleams of white through the dark green and grey of the forest and fjeld. To the north far below in the valley is Aakre Vand, a beautiful irregularly shaped lake dotted with fir-clad islands; while beyond, high up, there can be just distinguished Aakre Sæter, and frowning over it the dark mass of Aakre Kampen, a mountain of considerable height. Aakre Vand is a lake that we had intended to fish after Slangen Vand, but as there seemed to be no possibility of getting our property from one to the other we gave up the notion. According to all accounts it is a good lake for fish, and its shores are untainted by the habitations of man.

We started about 9.30, having paid 5*s.* 6*d.* for the board and lodging of ourselves and our numerous retinue, including the price of a sack-full of hay for our beds, as this was the last place at which we expected we could get any.

After watching for a short time our valuables jolting, plunging, and splashing over the uneven ground, covered with rocks, junipers, and occasional logs and brooks, the wear and tear on our heart-strings became too severe, and we decided to walk on to Sikkildals Sæter, about four miles, and leave the baggage to its fate under its guidance of our three charioteers. It took us till eleven o'clock to get within half a mile of the sæter, and there we sat down and watched the track intently for two hours: then two hours more—and we began to lose patience; then another hour—and we began to lose hope also. Something must have happened; either a canoe was smashed, or washed away crossing a stream, or one of the sleighs was upset and broken, or they were bogged, or the man carrying the bag had fainted, or his pony become unmanageable and dashed through a shop window; or, most dreadful thought, the men had got at our whisky and become hopelessly drunk.

Another hour passed, and our small remaining stock of good temper went: we were very hungry, and all our food was on the sleighs, and the mosquitoes seemed to be even more hungry than we were. Hope deferred, with nothing but mosquitoes to distract one's thoughts, maketh the heart very sick indeed: and these were most annoyingly large mosquitos; the finest brand that we have yet inspected, and with more strength of character than the ordinary kind. We were so much annoyed with the world in general, and each other, that we were obliged to separate, and Esau retired for a short time to attempt a sketch. He came back very angry, because just at the critical moment a mosquito had knocked his hat

off, and he had had a desperate and perspiring conflict with it under a tropical sun; but eventually the brute was vanquished and its head cut off, which he said he would have stuffed, to hang up in his ancestral halls. He certainly bore on his face the marks of the struggle, so that there seemed to be no reason to doubt the story.

Our state of despondency waxed worse and worse; we had not the slightest confidence in our head driver; he was undoubtedly the Svatsum village fool, for he talked all day, and the other men went into roars of laughter at whatever he said, though the Skipper said *he* couldn't see anything funny in most of his remarks; but possibly the Skipper was jealous because this man made better Norsk jokes than his own. Besides this, the fact that neither of us understood the language detracted from the merits of the jests.

Years rolled away, and at six o'clock something came slowly into sight. 'Out with the glass!' (the spy-glass). 'Yes, by George! it is the men and sleighs at last. Out with the other

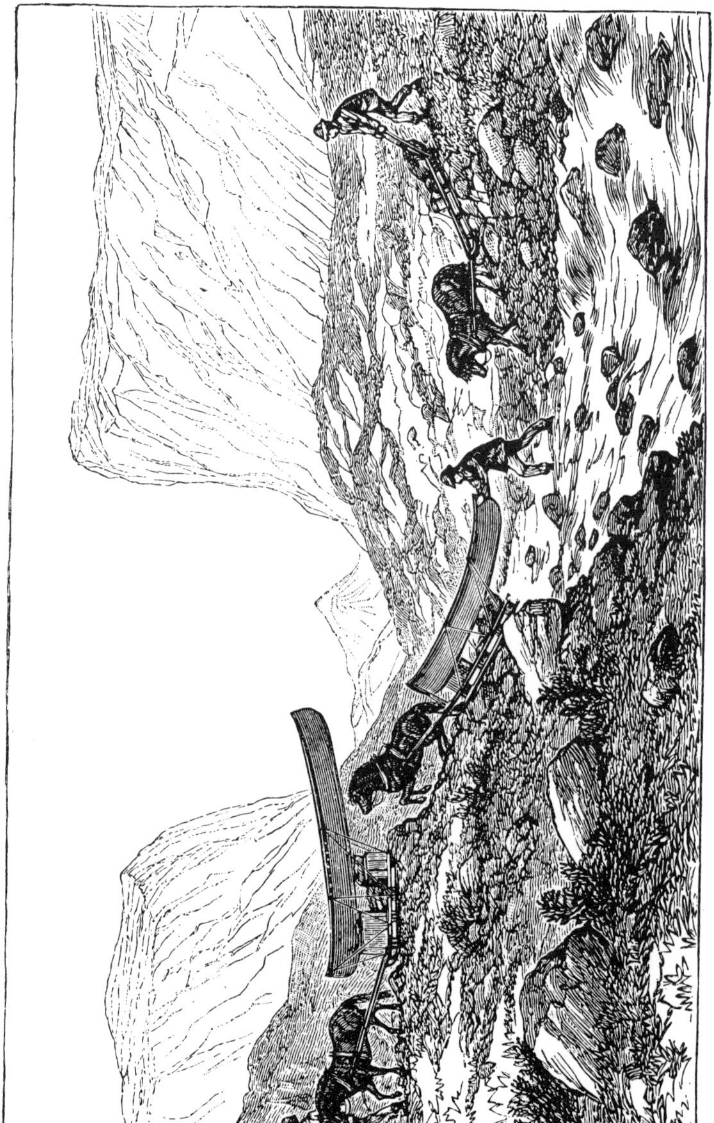

glass!' and we finish the 'wee drappie' that we were saving to the last extremity. They soon arrived at Sikkildal Sæter with us, and we found that nothing had gone wrong, but the men had been *very* careful, and so had taken nine hours to make a journey of four miles. The track certainly would be a disgrace to a Metropolitan Vestry, and they managed well to arrive with everything uninjured. We consider the village fool to be a most painstaking and praiseworthy idiot.

At Sikkildal Sæter we got some food and called at a small house close to it, where a Mr. B., a Norwegian barrister, was staying for the summer. He is the owner of the Sikkildal Lakes, and we wanted permission to camp on his land and fish in his lakes. He understood English as well as all the upper classes in Norway do; and was very civil, giving us the permission most willingly.

We have heard from a good many people that the wealthier Norwegians do not like the English, and will not do anything to oblige them; but in all our wanderings we have met with nothing but the greatest kindness and hospitality from all classes. Several people have gone out of their way to voluntarily offer fishing and shooting, and in no instance has the slightest incivility been shown. Certainly Norway will compare with England very much to advantage in this respect, though of course we do not mean to say that similar conduct would be possible in England.

At about seven in the evening we got all our cargo shipped again and started up the lower Sikkildals Lake—having first paid our charioteers £3 for the trip from Olstappen, three men, horses and sleighs, sixteen miles over the rockiest, brookiest, and juniperiest country in this world, and offered them whisky and water all round, including two men from the sæter who came to our assistance when the smallest pony, not being accustomed to the deceitfulness and treacherous wiles of this life, got up to its neck in a bog close to the lake, and the man with the bag followed it. However, they were extricated with no damage done, as our provisions were all securely soldered up in tins. Curious to relate, our three men did not like whisky, but just sipped for 'manners,' and only the two old men from the sæter would drink it; but these two old men liked it very much, and drank all they could get—that is to say, their own glasses full, and the other fellows' glasses full, and just a drop after that, and then just a taste to top up with. Then we shook hands all round, and feeling in charity with all men, sailed joyously away up the lake.

It was a real Norwegian night, with the warmth and light of the departed sun still lingering on the mountain tops, and a midnight twilight glowing in the valleys. We had a beautiful full moon to help us on our way, so we went right to the upper end of the first lake, and found a camping-ground half-way between the two lakes, which are about a hundred yards apart. The portage took us some time, but we were full of energy from the cool night air, so refreshing after the long hot summer day. We dug out a nice level place for the tent, and got everything settled and ourselves in bed about midnight.

CHAPTER IX.

SIKKILDAL.

Sunday, *July* 25.—We arose soon after seven; not because it is our nature to get up at that time, still less because we think it our duty to do so; but because the sun made the tent so intolerably hot that there was no pleasure to be derived from staying in bed any longer. Naturally after this we were very cross, which the Skipper says all really pious people are on Sunday morning; and he abused Esau shamefully, because the latter wanted the eggs buttered and the Skipper wanted them fried. Altogether we made ourselves as disagreeable as possible to each other—just as we do in our happy homes on the Sabbath morn in England. Fortunately Sunday only comes once a week.

Breakfast over, the Skipper devoted himself to the occupation of greasing his boots and shaving, which he seems to do at the same time, so that one brush may be used for both the soap and the grease; while Esau did some washing.

We had some trouble in getting good firewood, for Sikkildals Vand is more than three thousand feet above sea level, and consequently we were above the region of pine forests, and had only the stunted birch and juniper from which to obtain our supply. We divide the altitudes rather differently from the system adopted by other great explorers. The lowest belt is that of pine forests and strawberries, then comes the zone of stunted birches, above that only juniper and bitter willow are found; and the highest belt of vegetation contains only rocks, reindeer-flowers, and moss, and then eternal snow.

Now birch-trees do not make good firewood, for when they die they appear to get water-logged, and never burn well. The juniper is the most invaluable of all trees, for it will burn quite green; but at Sikkildals Vand it is very scarce, and so it took us quite a long time to collect enough dry wood to last our stay out, but it was done at last. We carried one canoe across the spit of land between the two lakes, and in it the Skipper went forth to get fish for the larder, while Esau took the other canoe down the lower lake to get some milk from Sikkildals Sæter.

The scenery here is very fine. The lakes are narrow, and highish mountains rise on each side: those on the south side had snow upon them, though this would disappear before the end of the summer, as we are not yet in the regions of perpetual snow; on the north side there is a very remarkable mountain called Sikkildals Horn, with a perfectly impracticable front of overhanging rock, very high and rugged. There was a constant rumbling and booming proceeding from it, as rocks from time to time broke off and came crashing down; but our tent—though seemingly under this cliff—was well out of their reach. At the further end of the upper lake we could see an apparently impassable mountain ridge. Beyond this, about four miles further according to the maps, was Besse Sæter, a farm, or ranch, only one day's journey from our final resting-place. How we were to cross that mountain with our canoes and baggage was a matter only to be determined by prophets and other beings of a higher order of intelligence than ours. Our friend Mr. B. thought it was almost impossible; the Skipper boldly asserted that it *was* impossible, and requested to be allowed to die here; while Esau, with the sanguine joyousness begotten of total ignorance, said of course it could be managed. We determined to move to the end of the lake the next day, and try the pass on the one following—barring earthquakes.

Esau had a most interesting voyage. His fishing was not very successful at first, and he paddled steadily on towards the Sæter, overtaking a boat quite full of girls, dressed in the very picturesque native costume which the people in these primitive regions still adhere to, especially on Sundays. The girls about here are rather pretty than otherwise, and these

were a particularly good selection, and of course all in their cleanest and smartest clothes for Sunday. They *would* stop to watch him fishing, till he got quite shy, and gave up throwing till they rowed on.

Soon he came to a brood of pochards under the leadership of the old duck, and spent half an hour trying to capture one by rapid paddling, in which endeavour he was nearly but not quite successful. There were a good many teal and pochards on the lower lake, and plenty of sandpipers on the shores of the upper one.

At last he reached the Sæter, and found there all the girls of the boat, and at least another boat-load and five or six strangers—quite a crowd; possible they had been having a church service, but probably not, as they all seemed in the best of tempers, and were most amiable.

He got the milk, and coming back tried a few casts, and found that the fish were rising properly; the result was nineteen good trout in about an hour and a half. We had not been catching many fish lately; so after his return to camp we concluded that this was the hour and we were the men to revel in a fiendish glut of capture. So there was a regular stampede in that camp, and after dinner we *all* went out armed to the teeth with rods and fly-books, and clothed in landing nets and Freke bags, with our teeth firmly set and a bloodthirsty look in our eyes, intending to struggle with the great trout in his native element or perish in the attempt. . . .

About ten o'clock that night there might have been seen toiling wearily back to camp under a cloudy sky and with a chilly blast a-blowing, two forlorn youths, 'sans' fish, 'sans' hope, but still armed to the teeth with the weapons of the chase.

July 27.—The day commenced with showers, and as there are no inhabitants here to whom we can give the surplus fish, we did not like to catch any more—for it is against our principles to waste food wilfully, woeful want being too near and probable a state to be trifled with—consequently we determined to move on, but first to bake some bread.

This, in a temporary camp, is done by putting the kneaded dough into a tin pot made on purpose without solder; this pot is then placed in a hole in the ground in which we have previously kept a good fire for about half an hour; before putting the pot in, all the embers and ashes are cleared out, and then raked back on to the top of the tin and all round it, and a small fire is kept going on the top. If well managed this bakes excellent bread in about twenty minutes, but of course it requires considerable experience and care to turn out really satisfactory bread. When we get to our permanent camp we we shall make a proper oven.

CHAPTER X.

BESSE SÆTER.

July 28.—Our two men arrived while we were at breakfast this morning, and brought two sleighs in the boat with them; these they deposited on the shore, and then one of them departed into some secret haunt of his own in search of a horse. The last we saw of him was a wee dot struggling up over the mountain crest; and we began to feel what a hopeless sort of task was before us.

When we had finished our breakfast there were certain remnants of food, and these we offered to the other man, because he seemed to want something to do. We left him in the tent with a frying-pan containing two trout fried in butter, and a tin pot nearly full of soup. Some time afterwards we looked in, and saw him eating greedily off his knife-blade, and after a further interval we noticed that he had finished; then we examined the culinary utensils out of which he had been feeding, and found he had left the trout untouched, but the butter they were fried in he had utterly consumed off the blade of his knife, and also all the soup through the same medium. But there was not more than a gallon and a half of the latter, so we did not grudge it.

Apparently he was like a giant refreshed after his meal, and seizing one canoe he carried it up to the top of the mountain, and then came back for the other and did the same with it; after this he returned again and borrowed our axe, saying he wanted to make the path better for the sleigh. He disappeared among the stunted birches, and we heard him chopping and slowly getting further up the track for about an hour. We naturally supposed that he was clearing away trees that ob-

structed the path, but when we came to traverse that path ourselves, soon afterwards, we discovered that he had only been filling up holes in the road by felling trees across it. Now a road that can be improved by this process is in a very bad state, and this one was decidedly improved.

Besse Sæter is only three miles from Gjendin Vand—the haven where we would be; and the snow-capped mountains, which have been gradually getting nearer all the way from Olstappen, are now magnificently towering above us on three sides.

The Sæter is a hut, built, as they all are, entirely of wood, and only inhabited during the summer months. The hut in which we are living is not strictly speaking a sæter at all, but has been built for the convenience of travellers, and the Tronhuus family are intrusted with the duty of taking care of those who come hither while wandering about this, the wildest and grandest part of Norway. The real sæter is a larger building about a quarter of a mile from this hut, and higher up the mountain. And further away still there is yet another building, or collection of buildings, also called Besse Sæter.

Our hut has three rooms, two of which—a bedroom and eating-room—are occupied at present solely by us: in the other room dwell two girls, apparently guests of the Tronhūus. Peter Tronhūus himself and his numerous family live in a one-roomed hut just opposite this. At present the family appears to consist of two men, five women, and two children, relationship to each other unknown.

Peter and his son Jens—who was with us on a former expedition—are both away at present; the latter engaged in procuring various articles for us, such as potatoes, men, ponies, and dogs, about which we wrote to him from England, and he is expected back to-morrow.

In spite of the crowd of people living here, everything is beautifully clean and tidy, and our eating-room looks very nice, with its floor always covered with fresh juniper sprays, and a cheerful fire burning in that most charming of fireplaces, the primitive Norwegian corner-hearth, which is being rapidly superseded everywhere by horrid tall, black, iron stoves, that look like coffins set up on end, and smell like flat-irons and rosin when they are lighted.

We shall have to make this place our home until Jens turns up; and we are not at all sorry to do so, for they take the greatest trouble to make us comfortable, and the trout, fladbrod, and coffee, are simply perfection. Besides, we are only a short day's journey from Memurudalen, where we intend to camp, and there is nothing to be gained by getting there before August 1, the opening day of the reindeer season.

July 29.—Jens arrived at breakfast-time, and after greetings had been exchanged, reported all his achievements on our behalf. He had secured for us a stalker, one Ola; a hewer of wood and drawer of water, by name Ivar (his last office seems likely to be a sinecure, but we can work him double at the first-mentioned employment), a horse, and a sack of potatoes; all of which will arrive at Memurudalen in time for August 1. We hoped for a dog for Ryper, but he had not been able to get one.

Esau is always bemoaning the law which prohibits him bringing dogs from England; it is suspected that he has a large collection of useless animals there, that he wishes to import into Norway and sell to the guileless and unreflecting native. Unassisted by any of the canine tribe, however, we have now accumulated what we call 'a good larder of bird-meat;' for certain wild fowl were observed to-day to secrete themselves in the marsh at the head of the lake, whither we followed them with all our dread artillery, and we now have a lot of teal, greenshanks, sandpipers, and a ring dotterel stowed away and engaged in preparing themselves by decomposition for our consumption. Some of these birds are almost unknown to the table of the ordinary Briton; but if he will consider that our daily food depends entirely on what we shoot or catch, we hope, as the writers of books say, 'the kind reader will excuse' the sandpipers and dotterel.

We were wet through on the marsh, and not at all sorry to return to a comfortable fire in a warm room, instead of the streaming sides of a cold and cheerless tent. Shooting as we did above our knees in water, the rain did not make any appreciable difference in our great wetness. After the point of saturation is past, we have discovered that the human frame is as impervious to moisture (external) as a macintosh.

This summer so far has been remarkably wet and cold for Norway, but we have now the inexpressible consolation of knowing that they are in worse case at home; for we have received our first batch of letters and papers from England, which have been a fortnight *en route*.

July 30.—We settled not to go to Gjendin ourselves to-day, as the weather was so very unfavourable, but we packed and despatched some of our luggage this evening, and purpose following it to-morrow.

Before doing this we had a long interview with Jens Tronhuus, with the main object of settling all accounts. Now a long interview between three men who cannot speak two words of each other's languages is a somewhat intricate business, and would be decidedly amusing to beholders. How we got through it is beyond the wit of man, but nevertheless the fact remains that everything is beautifully arranged; we thoroughly understand each other; both sides are satisfied; and we concluded everything without the aid of that potent mediator, Whisky, the Great and Good.

Besse Sæter grows upon one: the people are all so simple and kind, and cook our food so well, that we shall be quite sorry to leave, even though trout and reindeer are in prospect.

CHAPTER XI.

GJENDIN.

July 31.—The morning appeared rather fine, so we packed the rest of our baggage, and climbed the track which leads over the shoulder of the mountain between Sjødals Vand and Gjendin (pronounced 'Yendin'). It is rather steep, but nothing approaching the villainy of the tracks near Sikkildals Sæter, so the transit did not take long, and we got to Gjendesheim about twelve o'clock.

Gjendesheim is a very good two-storeyed wooden building, with a large dining-room, and about eight tiny cupboards of bedrooms, it has been erected just where the Sjoa River runs out at the eastern extremity of the lake, for the benefit of travellers, who can get food and lodging of a sort there, and generally boats to take them up the lake. Ragnild—the woman who presides over it—is very nice, kind, and attentive, and talks English well. Her latter qualification hardly gets fair play, as not many English people come here; and indeed the Norwegians who visit the lake are not very numerous. From the book we can only see two English names before us this year; and yet Gjendin is perhaps the most beautiful, certainly the wildest and grandest, lake in Norway, and is well worth a visit from any tourist who has time at his disposal.

It is eleven miles long; very deep; very blue; and on all sides rising sheer out of the water for from 1000 to 4000 feet are vast black mountains with snow-clad summits; for it lies in the very heart of the highest mountains in Norway. It may not unfairly be likened to an unfrequented and awfully desolate Lake of Lucerne.

At 3200 feet altitude it is of course above the fir-trees, and

only in a few sunny nooks along its sides can even stunted birches, juniper, and willow earn a precarious living. It is at these places alone that there is any exit from the lake; for along the greater part of its length there is no level place large enough to pitch a tent; no vegetation except berries and moss; and no possibility of scaling the frowning cliffs by which it is surrounded. But there is a great fascination in such a scene; and although its first appearance is almost repellent, every moment of gazing seems to increase its beauty and awe-inspiring grandeur.

At lunch here a great event happened; we had Salon øl (bottled beer), and immediately bought the whole remaining stock, consisting of six bottles. These we degraded by packing with the inferior baggage in the canoes, and commenced the final stage of our journey, or voyage—whichever is the right term.

About two miles from Gjendesheim, on the south shore, we came to a waterfall which runs out of a small lake lying a short distance away up in the valley. At the mouth of this fall was a small neat hut in which a Christiania professor had just taken up his abode for a few days' stalking; we stopped a few minutes to talk to him, and then paddled on, trying a few casts now and then until we came to Memurudalen—our intended camp.

It is about half-way up the lake on the north shore, and is a very pretty little valley, profusely supplied with edible berries, surrounded by thick birch covert, and with more grass than we ever expected to find at this altitude; but it is by far the most favourably situated bit of the Gjendin shores, as it is sheltered from the cold winds and gets the sun all day.

We found a remarkably nice level bit of grass, screened by a rocky bank, and with what the Skipper called 'a brattling brooklet' in front, about two hundred yards from the lake. There we pitched the tent and made everything comfortable, but of course we shall not decide whether to stay here or not until we have tested its capabilities as reindeer ground.

Beyond the purling streamlet, and about thirty yards from our front door, the Memurua River goes tearing down, the colour of dirty soap-suds from the mud which is ground into it by the mighty Memuru Glacier, whence it springs. This glacier is about three miles from us up the valley, but not in sight from our tent; in fact, the hills are so steep that we are quite shut in, and can see very little except the snow-fjelds and peaks just opposite to us across the lake. These peaks spring from the highest plateau in Norway, which has an altitude of about 6000 feet, and both the plateau and peaks are almost inaccessible to the hunter, as it is a day's work to climb them, and any one doing so would probably have to pass the night on the top. This is annoying, for it is a capital place for deer.

An ancient hunter, some years ago, spent a long time in conveying with incredible exertions to the top of the central peak, materials out of which he constructed a windmill, then he descended and never went near the place again, and his windmill scared all the deer away from that table-land, so that they frequented places where a man could get to them; and the cunning hunter was rewarded by many 'stor bocks' (big bucks). But now the windmill has been destroyed by time and weather, and we fear that the deer again roam there unmolested and unscared.

Sunday, *August* 1.—It is our custom to rise on this day singing, 'Come, rouse ye, then, my merry, merry men, for it is our opening day,' but on this occasion it would not have been appropriate. We were not at all merry, because it was Sunday, and raining; we were frozen in the night, our men and potatoes have not come, and altogether we could see nothing to be merry about, especially as, the opening day having fallen on a Sunday, we did not feel justified in going out to pursue.

So we devoted ourselves to the pleasures of the table. Last night we had dotterel and sandpipers for dinner, this morning greenshanks, which are very good birds indeed. There was also a large brew of a meritorious composition known as Skoggaggany soup; the name is a little difficult to pronounce, but the soup does not taste anything like it; it is merely the Norwegian for a scaup duck. In England people have been known to call scaups unfit for food, but here, under the

perfectly awful appetites that we have developed, the Skoggaggany soup has very little chance.

After trying unsuccessfully to catch fish, we walked up the valley after lunch to look for a hut which is marked on the Ordnance map, and to see if there were any better camping-ground than the place we chose yesterday. We saw some beautiful reindeer ground, but could not find the hut or a camp.

On our return we perceived two men loafing about the tent, who we naturally concluded were thieves and murderers, and the Skipper hurried on to do battle with them to the death for the possession of our greatest treasure, the Salon øl. But on his arrival the robbers did not fly, but stood and stared with their hands in their pockets; so he lifted his hat and said, 'Ola?' (for of course he might have been a Dook in disguise); and one of them replied, 'Ja;' and cordiality being thus established, produced the sack of potatoes and the cook, like a conjuring trick, from somewhere behind him, out of his hat or coat tails.

Then we went into all kinds of details with him about his and Ivar's wages, which he did not understand, and he replied at great length in Norsk, which we did not understand, and so the interview concluded to the gratification of all concerned. Ola is a big good-looking man, rather too much of a gentleman, we fear: but Ivar is without doubt a perfect ass, and will never be able to do anything in the way of cookery, except perhaps boil a potato, and even in that enterprise we consider it would be six to four on the potato.

CHAPTER XII.

THE CAMP.

August 2.—The ground that the Skipper tried to-day seemed a first-rate reindeer fjeld; this means an uneven tract of mountain country, too high for vegetation, except occasional reindeer flowers and patches of gentian, but not high enough to be entirely covered with perpetual snow: this fjeld—where it is not snow—is made of rocks large and small, from the size of a haystack to that of road metal, some of them firm, but mostly loose, jagged, and sharp; the winter snow and frost leave them in this condition by continually splitting and re-splitting them: they are dark grey in colour, and at a distance look almost black.

What the reindeer can find attractive in such a place, possibly some one can tell; we cannot. There is apparently nothing for any beasts of the field to eat up there; but if you do happen to find deer before they see you, they are certain to be feeding, and Esau thinks they are eating the rocks; but the Skipper says it cannot be so, and inclines more to the theory that they feed on their 'young,' like tame rabbits, or, possibly on their own blood, like the pelican of the wilderness. As for the reindeer flower, which is supposed to be their staff of life, it averages about half a stalk to the square acre, but possibly it is possessed of many highly nutritious qualities, and a little of it goes a long way. Anyhow they thrive on their food, whatever it may be; they are always very fat, and uncommonly good to eat when you chance to slay one.

After dinner we tried all this portion of the lake for fish without success, and coming back received the awful intelligence from Ola that there are no fish in any parts of Gjendin except the extreme ends, and the waterfall where Professor N. is living. This is a dreadful blow to us, for we always count upon fishing as our main employment, and fish as our staple food: and if we cannot get any here we shall have to leave. At present we have some which we brought with us from Sjødals, but when they are exhausted there will be a mutiny in this camp unless sport of some kind presents itself.

August 3.—A curious accident happened to-day; there was no rain. We have in vain tried to account for this phenomenon, and can only fall back on the somewhat unsatisfactory theory that it is all used up. Esau went after deer on the Rus Vand side, and came back very tired to dinner without having seen any, but reported fresh tracks; he was full of the glorious view that the fine day had given him. He had been close above the Memuru Glacier, which is a very large one, and stretching beyond it as far as the eye can reach is a sea of snow mountains, most of them peak-shaped, but some domes or irregular precipices with immense glaciers lying between them, and here and there the greenish-blue waters of a lake distantly gleaming in the sunlight.

It is curious to note how the north and east sides of every peak are torn and ragged, with huge masses of rock riven from them by the action of the weather, while on the south and west they are comparatively regular.

August 4.—The Skipper went on to Bes Hø stalking. This is a high mountain 7400 feet above sea level. It is close to us, between Gjendin and Rus Vand, and is one of the dome-shaped species.

The Norwegians call their mountains either 'Tind,' which means a cone, or 'Hø,' a round top; 'Piggin,' a peak rather more jagged than a Tind; 'Horn,' apparently one steep side and one more gradual; and 'Kampen,' apparently a rough hill with nothing striking about its shape. Most of the mountains round here are Tinden, the finest being Memurutind, Skagestølstind, and Glitretind, the last over 8000 feet, only surpassed in height by Galdøpiggen, which, though in sight of us, is beyond our reach.

From Bes Hø the Skipper got a good view between the storms of Gjendin lying encircled by its enormous steep black banks of snow-capped mountains, the whole of its eleven miles of length being visible at once. Its colour is a creamy greenish blue, caused by the snow-water which comes straight into the lake by scores of torrents, which collect it from the various glaciers. The Skipper, who is always bubbling over with poetic similes, said it looked like a cupful of very blue milk in a crease of brown paper; but beautiful as this idea is, who can take any pleasure in scenery without a little, ever so little, sport to flavour it withal? Certainly not the Skipper; so he came back from his long tramp disgusted with life, and longing to find that Esau had played the fool in his

absence, so that he might be able to pick a quarrel with him. Unfortunately Esau was provokingly amiable and had been performing acts of virtue, such as making soup, improving the tent, and swearing at the cook the whole day, so that the seething volcano of the Skipper's temper had to content itself without an eruption. We did manage to get up an approach to a row about the Memuru Glacier, which the Skipper had visited to-day; he described its beauty and the extraordinary blue of the ice, where the large crevasses near its lower end gave glimpses of its real formation—for of course it is covered thickly with snow except just where it begins to break up. Then he went on to say how curious it was to think that this huge mass, covering square miles of ground, is always moving onwards, and that no more powerful agent exists for altering the arrangement of the earth's crust than that cold, placid field of ice. Esau said it did *not* move. He watched it for half an hour yesterday and it never stirred, and he even pushed it with his stick without the smallest effect.

It is impossible to argue with a man of that kind.

We always do our baking just before bedtime, when the men have gone to their hutch, and in a permanent camp it soon gets reduced to a certainty. We prefer milk to water for mixing with the flour, as it makes the bread crisper and shorter and it does not matter how sour the milk is. This is most providential, as we have generally plenty of sour milk. We send twice a week to Besse Sæter, distant about eight miles, and the long journey does not agree with the milk, so that it is generally turned before it arrives here.

Another important article of food is soup, of which we have several varieties. When made of scaup duck, it is—as already mentioned—called Skoggaggany soup; but our present brew is 'gipsy soup,' which is made from potatoes, fishes chopped into small lumps, a square of 'Kopf's compressed vegetables' —a most invaluable article—and all the bones from the birds that we happen to be using. We never empty the pot, but keep adding water and bones as fast as we consume it, and it simmers by the fire all day. But when times are very bad, and we have no meat, and are living on fish, our soup is then called 'prairie soup,' and is composed of every scrap that we can collect—fish-bones; bacon; potatoes; milk; dandelion, and sorrel; bread, and biscuits: and whenever it develops any unusual flavour, we look suspiciously round to see if that boot-lace or candle-end is missing, or if any of the tent-pegs have been newly whittled. It is always very good, and we call it 'prairie' because of the dandelion, which is a prairie flower.

There is yet one more kind, known as 'Argonaut soup,' the recipe of which was introduced from America by the Skipper; but our resources have never yet been so low that we could not make something better than this.

Recipe for Argonaut Soup.

Take a pail of water and wash it clean. Then boil it till it is brown on both sides. Pour in one bean. When the bean begins to worry, prepare it to simmer. If the soup will not simmer it is too rich, and you must pour in more water. Dry the water with a towel before you put it in. The drier the water, the sooner it will brown. Serve hot.

CHAPTER XIII.

GJENDESHEIM.

August 5.—Such a lovely morning at last that we were quite tempted to stay, but nobly stuck to our resolve to go to Gjendesheim, heaped everything we possessed except rods, guns, and a change of raiment, into the inner tent, and covered them with a ground-sheet; then packed the selected weapons into the canoes, and sailed from these inhospitable shores.

Not far from camp we saw some fish rising under a cliff, and though it was a dead calm, and the sun as bright as sun could be, we stopped to try for them.

Esau soon tired of casting, and mentioning that 'if *he* could not catch those fish no one could,' paddled off to make a formal call on the Professor, and ask if he had got any deer.

The Skipper persevered, and was rewarded with two fish weighing about three pounds, and the most perfect fish for shape and condition that we have ever seen. This was an important event for us, for it entirely demolished Ola's theory of the non-existence of fish here, and gave us new hope for the future, especially as the weather has been so bad all the time until now, that we should hardly have caught any even if they swarmed.

The Skipper is devoted to the sport of 'throwing for a rise,' which he thinks the perfection of fishing. It can hardly be pursued with success anywhere but in Norway, for only there do fish seem to rise greedily after a constant succession of fine, hot, sunny days, with never a drop of rain or cat's-paw of wind.

The great charm to him is the extreme delicacy required. You *must* put on your thinnest cast, your smallest fly, and throw your lightest; and unless you throw a very long line you have not a chance for the beggar. Then, if he comes at you, you can see him through the calm clear water, and watch the whole performance. You get a rather better chance where two fish are rising close together, as there is some jealousy and competition between them, and each of them is likely to rush at your fly without sufficient meditation, lest the other one may get it first.

The Skipper has studied fish from a moral point of view, and says that they are very much like men: and he invariably turns his knowledge of their habits to good account. Throwing for a rise—in a lake like this, where the fish run large—on a calm bright day, is decidedly his forte; his motto in fishing

being 'far and fine.' Whereas Esau shines more in a rapid stream than elsewhere.

The latter had a great time with the Professor, who he said was a capital fellow, and gave him whisky, which they drank 'to better sport;' and they both agreed that there were no reindeer to be found in the district at present, and the Professor said he was going further north if matters did not mend speedily.

After the fishing and visiting were concluded, we hoisted sails of primitive construction, formed of a rug and a landing-net, which, with a fair wind, soon brought us to Gjendesheim.

We think this wind is the chief cause of our misfortune. When we were in these parts before, the wind was always against us whenever we journeyed; and in that year we had first-rate sport, both in shooting and fishing. But this time the wind has always been with us, and we pay for the luxury by getting no shooting and not much fishing. 'No mahtterr—a time will come.'

After food the Skipper with Ola went over to Leirungen—a small lake about three-quarters of a mile distant. Ola carried his canoe, and did not like the job. It gives us considerable satisfaction to make Ola do any work, he is so abominably lazy.

It seemed that the tide of luck was already changing, as both he and Esau—who was throwing a fly on the river nearer home—brought in a few nice fish.

Just before bedtime there arrived at the rest-house three Norwegian tourists of the sterner sex, and a young lady the daughter of one of them. The father was a barrister, and the other two were the Lord Chief Justice of what they imagine to be Common Pleas, and a very thin, dried-up student of theology. They all talked English, and the young lady seemed anxious to practise the language.

August 6.—After a gay breakfast Esau went his way to fish, while the Skipper—ever devoted to the fair sex—offered Miss Louise a cruise in his canoe.

The sun shone brightly as they moved over the quiet waters, and the fish were too lazy to rise, but lay idly thoughtful at the bottom of the lake. The Skipper was very polite to his charming companion, as she sat in a state of blissful comfort amongst the rugs which he had placed for her in the bows of the boat; and no sound was heard but the gentle plash of the paddle in the water, and in the distance the Sæter girl calling home the grazing cows.

But presently a cloud gathered over the mountain tops,

and thunder was heard rolling among the distant hills; a gentle breeze stirred the surface of the water, and every lazy fish woke up to seek his food. The Skipper longed to go and fetch his rod. He hinted at this, and at last became impatient; but, by Jove! Miss Louise would not go. There she sat and prattled on, charming, pleased with herself, and utterly unmindful of the rising fish and the fretting Skipper. Time kept passing on, till at length her father brought relief by appearing on the shore to call her in to dinner; but then the Skipper had to get his food too, and when he had bolted the humble but indigestible crust and cheese, and rushed out again to seize his rod, he found it too late, as the lake was now dark with clouds, and the fish had left off rising.

Soon after lunch it began to rain like a waterfall, and Esau arrived with a lot of fish—spoils from the Leirungen Ocean, and the result of Spartan indifference to the attractions of woman. There is a shining moral in this tale.

He also brought a romance about a rainbow, which had been so close to him that the two ends met at his feet. The rain hereabouts is very thick.

The evening proved too wet to fish, and this indefatigable young lady captured Esau, and after exhausting all the ordinary topics of conversation, began to show him every kind of puzzle that the mind of man ever conceived, puzzles with coins and puzzles with string; and she puzzled him with matches, and paper, and corks, till the poor young man became perfectly dazzled, and only longed for bedtime to put an end to his misery. Then she asked him riddles, first English and then French. The Skipper, apparently deeply interested in a book at the further end of the room, overheard Esau's answer to the first French riddle; it was 'Je le donne en haut.'

Presently, when they went up to bed, the Skipper said, 'I didn't quite follow your answer to that first riddle of hers. You said, "Je le donne en haut."' 'Oh! ah!' answered Esau. 'That's idiomatic French, and means a good deal that you don't understand; I always use it to gals, especially when they're pretty.' The Skipper coughed, and turned into his bedroom without saying 'good night.'

We have always been told that the Norwegian aristocracy particularly dislike the English sportsman in Norway. We think, therefore, that our fair friend cannot have been of very noble lineage. But she was very nice and rather pretty.

She left early next morning, and Esau said he was glad she was gone, as the Skipper was getting entangled with her.

CHAPTER XIV.

JOHN.

August 7.—We began another day by catching a beautiful bag of fish, and about midday were just starting to shoot our way over to Besse Sæter, when a man came in sight stumbling down the mountain track towards the rest-house. He was red and sunburnt, with a beard of about three day's growth. He was coatless, collarless, and apparantly exhausted. On his nearer approach we saw he was an Englishman, and presently when a few yards from us we recognised—John! Not the smart young beau we have always seen him in London; no longer the devotee to society and his club, but an almost unrecognisable John, so sunburnt and hot and hungry. Formal greetings were exchanged: 'Dr. Livingstone, I presume?' 'Mr. Stanley, I believe?' and we rushed into each other's embrace.

Then we besought him to refresh himself on fladbrod, milk, and coffee; which he did, largely. After this he became calm enough to give us a brief summary of his adventures since he left England.

He had done the journey from Christiania in very quick time, and had left all his luggage twenty miles behind at Hind Sæter, which is the nearest place to us to which wheeled vehicles can get. From thence he had started at five o'clock this morning. How he found the way is a marvel, but by great good fortune he met a man when he was about three miles out of the track, who put him right; otherwise he would probably never have arrived anywhere.

He has brought additional stores for the camp, as arranged before we left England, and we had left a note in Christiania asking him to call at the shop in Vaage, and try to get a small stove for the tent, or at any rate find out the price of one. Vaage is our nearest village, about fifty miles distant.

When John arrived there, seeing the shop as he drove past, he descended from his cariole and entered. The shop was full of people buying all the necessaries of life; for in these villages there is only one shop, which is a general store for everything. John was a little confused at his first experience of a Norwegian shop, but at last pulled himself together, and seeing a stove standing in the middle of the room, intended for heating the place, he walked up to it, and stroking it gently with his hand, looked round at the people generally and remarked, 'Hvor meget' (How much)? Dead silence not unmingled with awe followed this observation; for those simple rustics thought there was a maniac among them. This perplexed John, and as everybody was staring at him, and he began to find himself in a remarkably tight place, he concluded to make another remark, so asked in Norsk, 'Have you any whisky?' The storekeeper having no license looked horrified, and said 'Nei.' So John pursued his advantage by inquiring, 'Have you any aquavit?' 'Nei' was again the answer, and an ominous whisper of 'lensmand' (the policeman) was plainly audible. John thought he had asked enough about stoves to quiet his conscience, and guessed it was time to quit that shop. So rapidly regaining his cariole, he vanished before any of the crowd had made up their minds what to do.

We kept to our plan of going to Besse Sæter, starting as soon as John had finished his lunch, and got several teal and a greenshank on the way. On one little bit of water we spied three teal near the bank, and having both together made a most skilful stalk, got them all.

Sunday, August 8.—Our object in coming to Besse Sæter was to break the journey to a place called Rus Vand, where a Norwegian owns a lake and hut: it is distant about two hours' walk from Besse Sæter, and we had a letter of introduction to Mr. Thomas, the owner, which we were anxious to deliver, so as to obtain leave to fish in the lake, the western end of which comes to within walking distance of our camp in Memurudalen; and the fishing is remarkably good.

Therefore this morning we started to clamber up the steep mountain side that has to be crossed between Besse Sæter and Rus Vand, and skirting the shores of Bes Vand—which lies on a small plateau at the summit—we soon found ourselves scrambling down over the loose stones, and through the willow scrub that covers the uneven slopes approaching the east end of the lake.

From our side of the river—when we reached its banks, while a boat was crossing to fetch us—we saw several men, and a couple of English-looking setters, a pointer, and a target fixed up about 200 yards from the huts, so that the place presented a very sporting appearance.

Mr. Thomas received us very kindly, and at once gave us permission to fish in his lake. Both he and his wife spoke English perfectly, as did another lady staying with them, and as most emphatically did *not* another sportsman also living there.

CHAPTER XV.

BACK TO CAMP.

August 9.—The morning was again very wet, but we are men of great decision and firmness; what our friends call 'obstinate' if they are civil, and 'pigheaded' when they want to be disagreeable, as friends usually do.

Therefore we started for the camp after lunch: that is to say, the Skipper and Esau started, as John remained to await the arrival of his baggage, for which Ivar had been dispatched.

About two miles from Gjendesheim on the north side of the lake there is an apparently perpendicular cliff, half a mile long, and over 1000 feet high: this is called the Beseggen, and at the top of it lies Bes Vand, so close to the edge of the cliff that it seems impossible to believe that the lake is 1000 feet above Gjendin, with nothing but a narrow strip of rock to hold it within its bounds, and yet the books say it is so, and we always believe anything we find in a book. The cliff looks perfectly unscaleable, but we believe it has been descended twice by an Englishman who used to live here, and once by a Norwegian youth.

Bes Vand is so high that fish will not live in it; the professional liars of these parts say it freezes solid every winter, and kills any that have been put into it. It is a little difficult to believe this statement, as it is a large and deep lake; but John says that a man who will believe a guide-book can believe anything; so we all do our best to swallow it (the statement, not the lake; we have hardly enough whisky to make the latter palatable).

Gjendin is liable like all mountain lakes to be suddenly visited by squalls, so that we generally like to paddle pretty near the side, but on this voyage it was not safe to do so; for under the influence of the rain, which was coming down as if it had never done so before, stones and boulders were rattling and crashing down the sides of the lake, and plunging into it, in a most alarming manner; and as far as we could see, the steep black rocks were thickly streaked with white lines, denoting torrents rushing down in places where ordinarily none were to be seen.

Just as we were passing the Beseggen, a dull boom like that of a distant cannon was heard, and looking up we could see far above our heads a huge spout of muddy water shoot out from the cliff, carrying with it masses of stone and *débris* of all sorts; evidently some bank had given way under the increased pressure of this enormous rainfall. We thought for one brief moment that it might be Bes Vand let loose on us, for even in fine weather it can always be seen leaking through fissures in the rock, so narrow is the division between the two lakes, but we did not stop to ascertain where it came from.

It soon became necessary to land and empty the canoes, by reason of the heavy rain, the bottom boards being completely under water, though we had only been afloat for half an hour.

Just before we got to Memurudalen the sun came out; Esau had a chase after a black-throated diver that came up from a dive quite close to his canoe, and then we both fell to fishing and got several good fish. This is just our luck: we had left camp for the last few days on purpose to get fish for food; we had caught many and salted them, and brought back 40 lbs. weight with us in a large tin can, and then, behold! we caught fresh fish in a place where we were assured by Ola that there were none, not even salted ones.

We found the camp looking uncommonly pretty and comfortable, and all our things perfectly dry and nice. The sun shone, and blue sky appeared, so that hope, contentment, and joy reigned supreme, for we knew that it could not rain any more now for at least a month, from the way it stopped quite with a jerk as the supply ceased.

John spent his day at Gjendesheim in eating, drinking, and fishing, especially the two former amusements. Truly that is a glorious country where a man can over-eat himself three times a day, and never have indigestion!!

CHAPTER XVI.

TROUT.

August 11.—Last night at sunset we 'could not see a cloud, because no cloud was in the sky;' the distant mountains looked as black as coal, and the heavens were yellow-ochre colour; whereupon Ola committed himself to the statement

that the fine weather would now be a permanent institution. Consequently our life has once more resumed its proper phase of perpetual picnic, and we roam about without coats or waistcoats, or any other garments that seem superfluous unto us; and to John all garments except a landing-net and boots appear to be unnecessary incumbrances. Reversing the natural order of things, we put on all our available clothes when we go to bed, and peel for the day when we get up.

It is difficult to believe that only two days ago we were shivering with cold, wrapped in gloom and india-rubber clothing, and wet through all day, when now the horizon is dancing with heat, the lake is perfectly calm, with the high snow mountains mirrored in its blue depths, and we are delighting in every little bit of shade, having pawned our macintoshes and thrown the tickets into the glacier torrent.

That same stream has been a source of great annoyance to John during the night. He wants to have it turned off, because its roaring kept him awake, and he was going first thing after breakfast to see the turncock about it; but, of course, it is hopeless. The municipal arrangements here are much the same as in London, and that official cannot be found when wanted; so he will have to content himself with damming it.

The hot sun has brought out flies in great profusion; the fish are rising freely, and man goeth forth to his labour rejoicing, and cometh home with a heavy bag and a light fly-book, for the fish here seem to be all good-sized; and as we have to use the finest tackle and smallest flies, the odds are rather in favour of the finny prey.

We all went fishing, and made a very pretty catch among us, the Skipper securing the greatest weight, and Esau the largest fish, weight $3\frac{1}{2}$ lbs. The Skipper also made some interesting notes on the moral and physical characteristics of these Gjendin trout. He said there seemed to be three methods of feeding in vogue among them. Some were moving in a large circle about two hundred yards in diameter, and rising at very short intervals as they went—these never came within ten yards of the shore. Then there were some that were travelling along about a yard from the shore, and these seemed to be rising even more frequently than the others, as there were more flies close to the rocks than out in mid-ocean; and there were a few cunning old beggars that had got a comfortable hole under a rock which they did not like to leave, and only rose at longer intervals, as especially tasty morsels floated by.

All the fish, to whichever class of risers they might belong, often took the moving artificial fly in preference to real dead ones that were lying on the surface of the water close by: from which we opine that they resemble us to the extent of liking fresh food better than stale; for our flies had no attractive tinsel to commend them to the notice of an epicurean trout, being the best imitations we can manage of the predominant fly, which is a small dark-coloured winged ant, with a little reddish orange about the long black body.

These flies have but a brief and disastrous existence. They only flew for the first time this morning, most of them had died by noon—for the lake was strewn with their corpses—and the survivors were all worried and consumed by fish before nightfall. Luckily there are plenty more where they came from, and the process can be repeated on new flies to-morrow.

It is very interesting to catch a fish off these rocks on a perfectly calm day like this; for in the clear water you can see the whole of the struggle, from the moment the fish rises till he is lying panting and exhausted in the net. How beautiful a big fish looks when he first comes ashore! How brightly he shines in the sunlight, and how sleek is his portly person!

Even if you cannot see your fish rise and take the fly, you can soon tell by his behaviour whereabouts the needle will come if you succeed in getting him on to the weighing hook. A large fish very seldom rises with any dash or swagger, but just a smothered ripple; perhaps a glimpse of his nose as he sucks in the fly; and he moves as if he were a nobody: then when he feels the hook, there is none of that dash and wriggle that you find in a small fish, but generally a rush like a rocket towards the middle of the lake, making you tremble for the safety of your reel line, and after that a stately diving and calm, dignified resistance for five or ten minutes till he has to give in. Sometimes, though not so often, the rocket business will be repeated more than once and a fish that does this deserves to escape, and often gets his deserts. There is something very fine about the proud bearing of a big trout in difficulties; for here in the lake he has not the same chance as his relations in the running water at Gjendesheim.

The largest fish seemed to be those feeding in a circle, and it was one of these that Esau caught, which he said was the father of all fish. He lost another much larger—no doubt the grandfather of all fish. He said it weighed five pounds. It is an extraordinary piscatorial fact that the largest fish always do get away.

In the afternoon Esau commenced excavating the long-promised oven from the face of the little hill against which our tent is pitched. It stands about a hundred yards from our hall door, and is constructed chiefly of large stones and mud—clay not being obtainable—with a flue cut in the hill-side: a single stone acts as the floor of the oven, under which the wood-furnace is kindled, and a sod of turf, from time to time renewed, does duty as a door.

Dinner at seven.

John wishes that the *menu* should be occasionally inserted for the benefit of gastronomic readers.

Vins	*Potage.*	*Légumes.*
Tea.	Prairie.	Potatoes,
Beer.		Fried and Boiled

Poisson.

Fried Trout.

Entrées.

Sardines.

Gibier.

Teal. Greenshank.

Entremets.

Compôte of Rice and Wimberries.
Jam. Marmelade.
Whisky

After this Esau finished the oven, and accomplished a bake of bread therein, which proved so successful that on returning from fishing at about ten at night, we all turned our attention to the production of the staff of life, nor desisted from our labours till eleven o'clock, by which time there was a goodly show of rolls and loaves spread out, and we went to bed feeling that we had spent a glorious day.

CHAPTER XVII.

REINDEER.

August 12.—We wonder whether our friends in Scotland and Yorkshire have such a day as this: if they have, it is rough on the grouse.

There is not a breath the bottle-green wave to curl, and the sun shines as if Odin had redeemed his other eye.

The Skipper and Ola went forth to pursue, and walked over an enormous distance into the previously unknown region of Memurutungen. Up on the mountains life on a day of this kind is bliss; there is more air there than in the valley, and it is delightful to be far away from the busy world—consisting of your two pals and Ivar—below; surrounded by the snowy peaks and sky, with not a living thing save perhaps an eagle in sight.

In the middle of the day they came on fresh deer tracks, at which of course their flagging interest revived; and presently they descried, on a snow fjeld about a mile away, two deer 'scooting' over the opposite mountain side. These they followed and made a long *détour* to get the right side of the breath of wind that occasionally made itself felt up there, for the reindeer has probably the most acute scent of all the deer tribe. In the midst of this *détour* they suddenly came in sight of two other bucks, about 300 yards away, much finer animals than the first two; in fact, they had the best heads the Skipper ever saw. But luck was against him; they were wrong for the wind, and a puff came just at the moment, which carried the unwelcome intelligence to those deer that their hated enemy was upon them, and they departed round a corner at a rapid trot, and were no more seen. Then Ola looked at the Skipper

with a sorrowful shake of the head, and said, 'Meget store bocks!' (very big bucks), and the Skipper replied, with a still more portentous shake, 'Meget, meget.' So they were left with their mouths wide open, muttering, 'Meget, meget store bocks.' And after following the tracks some time without seeing anything more of the deer, they gave up the chase and returned to camp, getting home in a very exhausted state about 6.30.

At dinner John informed the company that his bath in the lake yesterday was the third of a series, the first of which took place in Montenegro, the second in Algiers, and now this in Norway. He calls this a humble tribute to the geniality of the English summer, and thinks that he may be termed 'a polyglot ablutionist.' Some of the sojourners in this camp say it may be so, but it does not speak highly for John's love of water when undiluted with whisky.

Subsequently we found that the bath which he swaggered

about only occurred because he fell off a rock into the lake, and so dabbled about afterwards while his clothes were drying, which does not take long in this weather. This also accounts for the condition in which he returned to camp, 'sans bags, sans shirt, sans everything,'—barring his boots.

Late at night Esau, who was up last, put his head into the tent to remark that there was a first-rate comet on view, but he was received with such execrations from the other two lazy people in bed that he thought it prudent to say no more about it, and not to look at it any more himself.

August 13.—We spent the morning making a meat safe. This meat safe consists of a hole in the ground, neatly flagged with flat stones, and walled with the same, and furnished at the top with a wooden frame, into which fits a lid with hooks underneath it for birds. The whole is covered with a piece of muslin to keep off the villainous bluebottles. The muslin was brought to make into mosquito nets inside the tent, but in this happy spot the 'skeeter' is unknown, the sand-fly very rare, and the great greeneyed Møge—which bites a lump out of your leg and then flies to the nearest tree to eat it-—is conspicuous by its absence.

We have always been very careful not to prepare in any way for game before it is killed, but this usually successful plan has been a failure this year, so now we are desperate, and have made a safe which will hold a reindeer, and probably with a little more bad luck shall even go out stalking with ropes in our pockets ready to tie up the animal when killed. We caught Ola a week ago carving a piece of stick into the double-ended thing that butchers put between the legs of sheep to keep them apart (name unknown), but we promptly seized it, and made it into the handle of a frying-pan. But who can escape his destiny? We hoped that we had averted misfortune, but the deed was done, and no doubt it was owing to this that the Skipper failed to get a shot at the 'store bocks.'

When John and Esau had finished the safe and succeeded in catching enough nice fish for the requirements of the camp, they were seized with the desire of making a good bath. We have no first-rate bathing-place near the camp, as the glacier-river has made the lake too shallow round its mouth, and it is some distance to where the shore becomes bold and rocky.

They selected a nice little stream on the hill just above the tent, and toiled like navvies there for about four hours under a blazing sun, excavating and paving with flat stones, making a most palatial bath in the bed of the stream; when behold, just as it was completed, to use the graphic language of one of the constructors, 'May I be dodderned, and doggoned, and dingblamed by Pike, if the blooming stream didn't cease to run!' It did just supply about a pint of water before it quite stopped, into which Esau's watch flew as he flung on his coat with some slight, and perhaps excusable, show of temper. A pint of water is not enough for a man to bathe in, but it is quite sufficient to saturate a watch, especially if a stone obligingly smashes the glass and makes a hole in its face, obliterating the vii. viii. and ix. at the time of its immersion. However, he dug the mud out of the works, filled them with Rangoon oil, and is under the impression that that watch can be made to go again, and that a new face and glass and silver case will make it look all right. He is of a sanguine disposition.

They returned to camp saying that it would be all right as soon as the first rain came, but they reckoned without their host; the stream came from a little snowdrift on the mountain, and next time that Esau went up there he found that the heat of the last few days had melted it all away; hence its sudden stop. It never ran again. Perchance some future traveller will find the bath ages hence, and rejoice in its luxurious arrangements. In anticipation of this John wrote the following beautiful lines on the most prominent rock:—

'Stranger, pause and shed a tear:
There used to be a streamlet here;
But seeing Esau strip to lave
His sordid body 'neath its wave,
All filled with shame and blushing red.
The streamlet left its gravel bed;
Its only wish from him to flee,
It ran away and went to sea.'

The Skipper returned rather late with some very good fish from our old lake Rus Vand, and dinner was consequently at the extremely fashionable hour of 8.30.

MENU.

Poisson.

Truite à la Norvège.

Gibier.

Teal en matelote de Bacon.
Pommes de terre sautéd in a frying pan.

Potage.

Skoggaggany.

Potage is frequently eaten last, for it keeps hot longer than the other dishes, and as we always feed in the open air in fine weather, they cool more quickly than in civilisation.

About nine o'clock a splendid display of northern lights was produced for our benefit, and we stayed up till twelve o'clock baking bread and gazing at the ever-changing beauties

of this glorious sight. In the course of conversation it transpired that the same thing happened last night in a milder form, and it was this that Esau had announced as a comet. Tonight he was immensely delighted with the show, because he says it will bring good luck; quoting 'Aurora bright, dear harbinger of dawn.' He said this was Shakespeare, and if Shakespeare called Aurora a 'deer harbinger,' that ought to be enough for us. The other two agreed, but did not believe Shakespeare ever wrote that, or anything like it. 'What play was it in?' 'Play!' said Esau, with the utmost contempt, 'you awful duffers, it's in the sonnets; I dare say you never read all of them.' This was unanswerable, for of course no one ever did read all the sonnets. But in revenge John composed some poetry about Esau, after the manner of Walt Whitman, he said.

If Walt Whitman ever wrote anything like this, he ought to be made to read it. We give a few lines:—

> 'Twas he who culled the bluest berry sweet,
> And with his jodelling made the heights reply
> To airs that oft have graced the music hall:
> Anon when work or sport was put aside,
> The fragrant omelette he would deftly roll;
> No better man to fry the curling trout,
> None with more appetite to make it scarce.
> When tired nature seeks repose in bed,
> To lie when others rise and calmly rest,
> He most surpassed the seven Sleepers' selves.
> This is the sort of rubbish men can write
> Who to inanity devote their minds;
> But not save great experience will suffice
> To do the trick; no amateur can hope
> To vie with those who've studied it from youth.'

And so on for pages.

On examining the diaries which we all keep, the following remarks on the aurora were found:—

No. 1.—By the Skipper.

'The heavens were illuminated by most brilliant northern lights, which flickered in a great arch over the starry sky.'

No. 2.—By Esau.

'A most glorious display of northern lights, huge bands of light across the sky; waving, flickering, and disappearing, then suddenly shining out again more brilliantly than before, while all the time straight streamers of light were shooting upwards from the horizon.'

No. 3.—By John.

'The glow of a remarkably fine aurora borealis, whose silvery shimmering shafts flickered incessantly all over the heavens in the most fantastic shapes.'

It will be observed that we all agree in the flickering, consequently you may bet it *did* flicker. But for this fortunate fact it would be hard to recognise the three descriptions as identical, and yet this is the way history is written.

CHAPTER XVIII.

SUCCESS AT LAST.

August 14.—This was a most eventful day in our quiet life, and one fraught with episode. For the first time there was a breeze, so the Skipper went out fishing, and John to practise canoeing in a wind, which is an art requiring considerable dexterity in these Canadian canoes. They are beautiful sea boats, and beat the 'Rob Roy' hollow for any purposes where room for baggage is required. In our two, which are only small, we have transported between 800 and 900 lbs.; but their worst feature is decidedly exhibited in a wind, for the broad flat bottom and absence of keel cause them to drift very fast, and make it difficult to keep them straight. It can only be done by paddling from amidships instead of from the stern.

Esau went out stalking, full of hope from the aurora and the favourable wind.

The Skipper was lucky and caught some very good fish, and then returning to camp constructed a most lovely wimberry tart. He had just finished the enclosure of the same in the oven, and was proceeding to remove the flour and ashes and other *débris* from his hands, while John reclined at his ease under an awning with our latest 'Field'—three weeks old—when they heard a hail overhead, and behold a swarm of visitors from Rus Vand! Mr. and Mrs. Thomas, Miss A—— and their friend F——, who is the most celebrated deerstalker in the country. He is reported to never miss a shot, and occasionally shoots flying ryper with a rifle.

They tumultuously demanded lunch, and the Skipper with John had a pretty busy time of it for about twenty minutes, and the wimberry tart had to be left to its fate in the sultry climate of the oven. Our larder just now is not well supplied with anything except fish; so that the utmost exertions could only produce a meal which to people who have had reindeer for several days must have seemed poor indeed. Fried trout, Skoggaggany soup, tea, beer, bread, biscuits, and marmalade, was the bill of fare, for there was no time to do anything in the 'gibier' line, birds taking some time to pluck and clean. However, to our guests there were some points of this meal decidedly worthy of attention, viz., the beer, marmalade, and bread: they have none of these at Rus Vand, as their attempts at bread have hitherto been failures, while ours has been very first-rate ever since the oven was built, and was much appreciated.

We have been informed that the proper thing in these days, when writing a book, is to recommend some condiment or patent medicine to the notice of the confiding public. As there is no chance of our meeting any Arab sheiks in Memurudalen, we have to fall back on this episode of the bread, and seize the opportunity to sing to the world the praises of 'Yeatman's Yeast Powder,' by far the best that we have tried, and invaluable on an expedition of this kind for bread, pastry, and pancakes. Now let old Yeatman send his hundred guineas, care of Esau, and we will see that they are devoted to a proper use.

About four o'clock the call came to an end, and our friends departed over the mountain to Rus Vand, at the west end of which they expected to meet their boat. Before going they made us promise to go and see them next Tuesday, and will send a boat to convey us down the lake.

Soon after six Esau came into camp in an offensively jaunty manner, followed by Ola with the heads and skins, and what the lawyers call the appurts, to wit, the heart, kidneys, feet, and liver of two reindeer bucks. Then was there great rejoicing in that little colony, and dinner was served and disposed of with light hearts, even the neglected wimberry tart being a complete success, for owing to its gigantic size, its long baking in a cooling oven had not been too much for it, and it was finished to the last crumb of paste and spoonful of juice.

Our custom is, when a man returns with deer, that he shall lie on the sheepskin of indolence if so disposed, while the other fellows prepare dinner; and after the meal is finished and men are beginning to lean back and fill their pipes, he is expected to relate his adventures without interruption; after this he is never to refer to them again unless specially requested. Now for Esau's story.

'We went on to Memurutungen and began to find fresh tracks and signs of deer almost directly, so were on the tiptoe of expectation all the morning. About midday Ola found two deer on a small patch of snow, five or six miles from camp, in a very favourable place for approaching them, with the wind as right as it could be. We made a lovely stalk; but when after an hour's creeping we got to the spot, we were

just in time to see them disappear, slowly feeding over the hill. We followed as fast as possible, and soon came in sight of them again, for as the deer always feed against the wind there is no danger of alarming them by following on their tracks. A few minutes of breathless crawling like serpents, and we were within 100 yards, nearer than I ever got to reindeer before. One of them soon gave me a nice side shot, and when I fired he almost fell, but recovered himself, and they both ran down the hill towards a little glacier. I fired again at him and missed; and then ran as hard as I could towards the glacier, cramming in cartridges as I ran. They were both out of sight for a moment behind some rocks, and then the unwounded one came into view again, and I had a nice shot at him at about 150 yards, and was lucky enough to send a bullet just above his heart, which killed him instantly at the edge of the glacier.

I ran straight on, and following round the shoulder of the hill, saw the other one standing about 100 yards away, unable to go any further. I was in about the same state myself, so sat down, took as careful an aim as I could, and fired a shot which finished him. How he had ever got so far is a mystery, as the first shot only missed his heart by about an inch. The second went in touching the hole made by the first, and killed him at once.

'We gralloched them, and built the meat up with stones to preserve it from ravens, and the great bugbear of hunters, the "jarraf," as they call it; filfras is its English name. I think it is identical with the North American wolverine or glutton.'

The lecturer concluded his observations amid great applause.

Let it be understood that the running which is done in pursuit of deer is a gymnastic performance of the utmost difficulty, for these mountains are almost entirely composed of loose stones with sharp, clean edges. These stones vary in size, but otherwise are all similar, and have no more tendency to stick together and lie quiet than the lumps in a basin of sugar. So that running over them means—for an extremely active man—a pace of perhaps four miles an hour; for a deer about six or seven. Consequently the deer always when disturbed try to get on to snow, for there they can go a great, but unascertained pace—apparently somewhere about eighty miles an hour.

We find that after all we were quite right to make the meat-safe before killing the deer, for we only made it to hold one, and now we have killed two, and so are properly behind-hand with our arrangements, and shall be obliged to make another.

After dinner Esau went down to the lake and tried a few

casts from the shore. He speedily hooked a fish, which he thought the biggest ever made, and never got a sight of it for twenty minutes. He thought this a grand top up for a truly successful day, but on landing it, it only weighed a pound, but was hooked in the tail, hence the struggle.

CHAPTER XIX.

GJENDEBODEN.

Sunday, August 15.—Still the same beautiful weather. We spent the morning fishing and bathing. Esau distinguished himself by falling into the lake off a cliff, just as he had finished dressing after a bath; nearly swamping his canoe, full of fish, rugs, and other valuables. There was such a sun that he merely hung his things on the rocks and went on fishing without them until they were dry, which took a very short time. He always had savage tendencies, and would like to live without clothes, but we consider this is not dignified, and will not tend to promote discipline among our retainers. The Skipper got the best bag, as he generally does on a calm day.

After lunch we packed our rods, fowling-pieces, and change of raiment into the canoes, and started on a voyage of discovery up the lake, intending to spend the night at Gjendebod—a hut at the western end somewhat similar to Gjendesheim at the eastern, though not so large or so well built, for the upper end of the lake does not get as many visitors as the lower.

The expedition commenced with a disaster, owing, no doubt, to its being Sunday. As John and Esau in the larger canoe were crossing the glacier stream, something caused the boat to almost swamp, but fortunately right again with a good deal of water in it. Esau said it was John's clumsiness; John said it was Esau's recklessness in crossing at such a rapid place, and much recrimination ensued. They went to shore and emptied the water out, and then continued the voyage, nothing being wet except the rugs used to kneel on. Only the Skipper lingered on the voyage to fish; the other two paddling against a heavy head wind completed the journey of five miles in about an hour, and had dinner cooked and ready by the time the Skipper made his appearance with a beautiful basket of trout.

August 16.—After breakfast we found a drover, who was living in a hut here, and impressed him to come out with us after ryper—his function being that of the dog.

Our drover, however, was rather a great man, living in a hut with a real door and a window, and a live woman inside to cook for him and iron his shirt—at least, we imagined she must be doing this, as he had not got one on.

Ryper[1]) shooting began by law yesterday, but our Sabbatarian proclivities prevented us from going forth to the chase. The true reason is that we superstitiously believe it will rain again if we shoot on Sunday, though no one will confess that this is the feeling by which we are possessed.

We crossed the lake in the canoes—the Skipper and Esau to shoot, John and Herr Drover to beat. There was a narrow belt of birch trees between the lake and the willow belt in which we hoped to find the birds, and before we got through this, our ears were gladdened by the sound of two shots from Esau, who had walked on to two old birds and got them both; but alas! disappointment was in store for us. We walked up hill and down dale, dry ground and marshy, willow belt and birch belt, but never saw another ryper for five hours, and then we put up one old cock who fled away with a derisive crow before we got within sixty yards of him. It is hopeless work hunting ryper without dogs. We found plenty of places where they had fed or sat, or been running on wet ground; but they hate flying unless they are compelled, and on a day of this sort lie like stones, though we have seen them after windy weather get up almost as wild as Yorkshire grouse. But we feel that we have done our duty in trying to shoot ryper, and so now can go back to our fishing and stalking with a quiet conscience.

And if we got no more ryper we found such a quantity of 'moltebær,' that there is every prospect of Esau being seriously

[1]) Rype (lat. lagopus): A sort of ptarmigan, white in winter, brown in summer. Weight 1–1,2 lbs.

ill for some days, which would be a distinct gain as far as the consumption of our stores goes. The 'moltebær' is a berry like a large yellow raspberry, very good indeed to eat, with a sort of honey flavour about it. The Norwegians think it better than the strawberry, though we hardly indorse this opinion. It is a beautiful scarlet before it is ripe, and a dirty pale yellow when ready to gather. It grows low down, and is difficult to find, as it conceals itself in low, swampy, and rather dark places.

When we returned from the pursuit of the disobliging ryper, there was a fair breeze down the lake, so we hoisted sails and were soon back at Memurudalen.

CHAPTER XX.

A FORMAL CALL.

August 17.—This was the day appointed for our visit to the Thomas's at Rus Vand, but though we told Ola as usual to call us at 7.30, he never came until about half-past eight. His watch is a curiosity among bad watches; he sets it by one of ours every night, and it has always gained or lost several hours before morning: on one occasion it actually lost nearly a fortnight while we slept.

We started up the mountain at half-past ten, and arrived on the shores of Rus Vand very hot and tired in about two hours. There we saw a dim speck on the distant horizon which we imagined to be the boat coming to take us down the lake. So we began to fish till it should arrive; and it was a considerable time before we realized the fact that the speck we had seen was indeed the boat, but it was *going*, not coming, for the soulless wretch who had control of it had presumed to think, and his thoughts being of course the mere unreasoning impulses of a brutish and degraded mind, had caused him to suppose we were not coming. This was a terrible blow, but at last we bravely decided to walk on to the hut—about eight miles. During the next six pages of this book we walked and walked and walked, with hunger and thirst raging inside us, a broiling sun over our heads, and the most frightful language proceeding from our lips; tramping along cattle tracks, wading through mountain torrents, and stumbling over willows and rocks, till about half-past three in the afternoon, when turning the last corner we came on the two huts, and our olfactory nerves were greeted by the welcome scent of adjacent cooking food.

Thomas was most profuse in his maledictions of the idiot who had left the west end of the lake without waiting for us, and we had great difficulty in persuading him not to shed his blood there and then. Thus far the misery.

But now a change came o'er the scene. Behold the wearied travellers lying on the sward, in the cool shadow cast by the hut; surrounded by iced whisky punch, brandy and water, rum and milk, and claret, and drinking them all at once under the entreaties of our hospitable entertainers. Anon a sumptuous feast was spread under the canopy of a tent pitched just above the roaring waters of the Russen River where it leaves the calm of the lake for the turmoil and trouble of a hurried descent to busier regions. That trout, reindeer, roast ryper, and the various smaller birds will be remembered by all of us as long as we live.

August 18.—We all stayed at home to-day, as the weather—although still perfectly fine—was not favourable for any sort of sport with which we are acquainted except kite-flying; and the tent was constantly in such imminent danger of being blown from its moorings, that we feared if we went away, we should not be able to find it when we came back.

The Skipper and John devoted themselves to baking, and produced an enormous quantity of bread and biscuits; and when these were finished the united strength of the company engaged itself on a meat pie.

The divison of labour in this enterprise is always managed thus. Esau is butcher—an employment in which he revels, and at which he is decidedly an adept. He cuts up reindeer in convenient slices for placing in the pie-dish; adding thereto slices of bacon, and two or three hard-boiled eggs, with some liver, heart, and birds if we have any to spare. Meanwhile the Skipper concocts the dough for the crust from flour, butter, and boiling water; and after rolling the same on the top of one of the boxes with an empty beer-bottle, neatly lines the smaller of the two low tins with it; fills it with the various ingredients and plenty of pepper, salt, and some water, and then covers it with a thin disc of paste perforated with holes, and adorned with fantastic images of reindeer and birds. Now the pie is ready for the oven—which all this time John has been stoking indefatigably with arm-loads of wood; and when he announces that the oven is fit the pie is borne in solemn procession to it, and safely enclosed by the sod which acts as the oven door, and conceals it from our gaze for a time, which varies according to the size of the pie and heat of the oven.

We have some difficulties to contend with in the top of our oven, for the sods which fill in the holes thereof are liable to crumble with the intense heat and fall down in fine dust on our food gently stewing in its cosy nest. The only way to

obviate this is to water the top of the oven every morning as if it were a spring garden, and then the clods never get dry enough to play their evil little games. The Skipper compares the baking of a pie to burial by cremation (if that is not a bull). Certainly it always comes out etherealised; a thing of beauty and a joy for at least two days. Esau called this pie after its resurrection 'a harmony in yellow and brown quite too too utter and distinctly precious;' and John added, 'Begorra, me jewel, it is that same, bedad.'

We shall now be free to do what seems good in our eyes for several days without the trouble of baking: altogether our stock of provisions is enormous. This is always the way in camp life; first a week of existence on the verge of starvation, and then a time of milk and honey and tables overflowing with plenty.

August 19.—Some of the bread that John makes is rather heavy. Yesterday we were constrained to point this fact out to him. He pretended not to be able to see it, and in support of his theory ate at supper a quantity of the rolls that we had condemned. The consequence was that about two o'clock A.M. we were roused from our peaceful slumbers by John jumping spasmodically out of bed and rushing to the tent door, uttering at the same time most ghastly yells. At the door he appeared to be awake, so we said, sitting up in bed with our hair on end,—

'*Now* then, John. What's the row?' To which he answered very quietly,—

'Why, my line's caught on that rock over there. I wish you would stop the boat a minute.'

Then he went gently to bed again and continued his unbroken slumbers.

A sleeping man is selfishly regardless of the disquiet he brings on his fellow-creatures, and John, although he must have dreamt all sorts of funny things, did not dream that he was disturbing our night's rest.

The Skipper went after deer, but only had a very long walk without seeing any. We have now got the kitchen into a great state of perfection, so that within ten minutes of his return a recherché repast was on the table. This is rather a difficult thing to manage, as we never know to within a couple of hours what time the hunters will return; but it can be done by having the chops, steaks, or birds ready in one frying-pan, the trout in the other, the potatoes partially cooked and the tea or coffee made: the leaves or grounds of the latter we remove always after eight minutes' brewing, so that it does not alter by standing. The table of course is ready laid. Once and only once there was a long delay, owing to a misfortune with the water that had been boiled for the tea; but the explosion of wrath from the famishing hunter on that occasion was so dreadful, that the utmost endeavours have since been successfully used to prevent its recurrence.

MENU.—August 19

Potage.

Mulligatawny.

Poisson.

Truite à la Maitre d'Hôtel

Entrées.

Venison Pie.

Rôts.

Venison Pie.

Gibier.

Venison Pie.

Entremets.

Pancakes.

Our procedure with pancakes is for every man to fry and toss his own; the frying of the first side is easy enough, but the tossing requires skill, for we do not allow the mean practice of helping the delicacy over with a knife, indulged in by some weak-spirited cooks.

John's first became a mangled heap of batter under his repeated efforts, and was finally eaten by him in that condition; his second ascended towards the heavens most gracefully when he tossed, and was absent for some minutes, but unfortunately he failed to hold the pan in the right place on its return, and it fell on the ground, where it was immediately seized and devoured by Ivar. The third was a complete success, and so were the fourth, fifth, sixth, and seventh; the eighth stuck to the pan, and was a failure; and after that he got along all right to the thirty-fourth, when he had another partial failure, owing to over-confidence. This made him more careful, and all the rest were quite perfect. When we had finished we gave the rest of the batter to the men, who fried it all in one huge pancake, about two inches thick.

We notice that all the diaries agree for once; the following note occurs in all:—

'Pancakes for dinner to-day; the other two fellows over-ate themselves.'

We told John this morning of his adventure with the boat and fishing line during the night, so he ate all the new bread at lunch, thereby laying its restless spirit long before bedtime; no doubt he and his dinner will slumber more peacefully to-night.

It may be remembered that we brought a lot of fish slightly salted with us from Gjendesheim. Ever since our return here we have caught plenty of fish every day, and as we prefer fresh food to salt, the Gjendesheim fish which were placed in a little barrel have been neglected. Five or six days ago we noticed an unpleasant odour, and found that it proceeded from this barrel, the fish being in an advanced stage of decomposition, and the men told us they were making 'raki fiske,' a thing which they informed us in Norwegian is 'real jam.' We were very angry, and gave orders that the whole thing should at once be thrown into the glacier torrent. After this the affair faded from our minds, but yesterday we again noticed a suspicion of the same smell, and this morning it was so powerful that we began to invent theories to account for it.

John, who is a man of great scientific attainments, proved

to his own complete satisfaction that it proceeded from the bodies of prehistoric reindeer which had been engulfed by an avalanche ages ago and entombed in the glacier until now, when at last their decaying corpses were being washed down the stream.

He said Huxley had often observed the same thing and told him about it.

Esau's theory was that the glacier itself was decomposing. 'Look what a long time it had been standing exposed to the air, and most likely in a damp place; everybody knew that snow water was not good to drink, witness the goître of Switzerland; and why was it not good? Simply because it was putrid, and now that the hot sun was shining upon it, no wonder it smelt a little.'

He concluded his remarks by inquiring who Huxley might be, and was just setting off up the valley with a bottle of Condy's fluid to pour over the glacier, when the Skipper, who had wandered down to the Memurua River instead of arguing, suddenly rushed back with his fingers tightly holding his nose, and shaking his fist at Ola, said something that began with 'Dab,' and went on with other unknown words.

At last we gathered from his expressions that the barrel of 'raki fiske' had not been thrown into the torrent at all, but our villainous retainers had secreted it near the stream, intending to have a feast as soon as it should have become rotten enough to please their cultivated taste. Truly a Norwegian has the nastiest notions of food. Now the 'raki fiske,' barrel and all, is buried a yard deep, a long way from here, and life is again pleasant, but we have little doubt that Ola and Ivar will come back and root about and dig it up after we have left the country say a month hence: it ought to be in perfect condition by that time.

CHAPTER XXI.

FISHING.

August 20.—The first thing this morning we sent Ola to Gjendesheim with some venison for the people there, who have been very kind in sending milk, eggs, rice, onions, &c., to us. We have more meat than we shall be able to eat if the weather continues as fine and hot as it is at present.

We three walked over the mountain to spend the day at Rus Vand, taking our lunch with us. We got there about half-past ten, and the fish were then rising well, so we separated and commenced fishing, the Skipper and John taking the north side of the lake, Esau the south. After catching a few fish the rise stopped, as it always does on these lakes about midday.

There is no doubt that on a Norwegian lake the fisherman should above all things 'make haste while the fish rise.' It is all very well for the ancient sportsman to remark, 'Take your time, my young friend, there are as good fish in the sea as ever came out of it.' It is no doubt true enough; but at this time of year they will not rise to fly for more than about a couple of hours twice a day, and if you do not make the best of your opportunities then, where are you ? Put yourself in the place of the fine old veteran three-pounder who has got into the habit of taking his meals at regular hours for fear of spoiling his digestion, and has selected the hours between 10 and 12 A.M. and 4.30 and 6.30 P.M., because he knows from long experience that these are the most likely times to find flies on the water. He has come in from roaming in deep waters to the shades of the rocky coast, and has a certain appetite to allay after his bath and morning stroll. There he

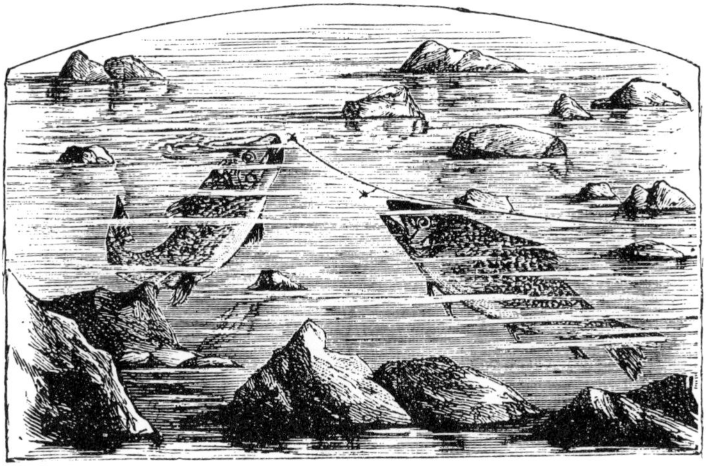

waits, and thinks of old times, and of how fat and shiny his tummy became the last hot summer there was, when flies were plentiful, and he had not to resort to this abominable device of catching small trout and eating mice[1]) to keep him in daily food, as he nearly always has to do now that the summers are so wet, and he is no longer active enough to compete with his younger relations in the struggle for existence. 'What times those were, and how he wishes he were a year or two younger again, and not crippled with useless length; and, by George! now he comes to look at his reflection against that stone, he's getting quite yellow and bilious under the belly, and'—— But he can't stop to moralise, there is a luscious March Brown of unusual solidity skating right over his pet

[1]) We have found as many as three mice in the stomach of a Rus Vand trout.

rock, and he can't let it pass. So up he comes and gulps it down with a lazy flop of his tail that leaves quite a swirl on the lake surface. 'Why, the thing's got no flavour, and how I've hurt my jaw with it!' Poor old chap, his day is over, and after ten minutes' struggle he has left his favourite haunt to be occupied by another tenant, and is safe in the landing net, a good three-pound fish, but, like most of those who have reached this size, not quite in as good condition as he was at 2½ lbs., and just a shade longer than he ought to be. Don't

stop to gaze at him, put him in the bag with all speed—it is necessary to hurry up and fish on while the rise lasts.

After weighing our catch, we cleaned them and cut off their heads to lighten them for the journey over Glopit, and even without this extra weight we were a good deal troubled and felt overburdened on the up-hill side, which is terribly steep and rough, only just practicable for a man on foot.

When we got back to camp we found that Ola had not returned from Gjendesheim, which caused us some sorrow, as Esau wanted to go out stalking on the morrow, and could not go alone. At least, he would be extremely unlikely to see any deer, for the reindeer being exactly the same colour as the mountains among which they live, it is almost impossible to see them before they see the enemy and depart hastily.

These native hunters are wonderful at the profession, and seem to know by instinct when they are in the vicinity of deer, as if they could feel their presence in the air. No doubt they really see indications that we should never observe, for they always begin to go cautiously, crouching and peering over rocks when deer are about, long before we amateurs are aware from the ordinary signs of footprints, nibbled reindeer flowers, or newly-moved stones, that there is likely to be any sport.

August 21.—It was cold and windy last night, so we turned into bed early and lay in luxurious comfort while John read out choice bits, all of which we know by heart, from the works of Mark Twain. We all think Mark Twain the best writer for camp life that has yet been discovered, and we have three or four of his books here. Besides these our library of light literature consists of Shakespeare, Longfellow, Dr. Johnson's Table-talk, and novels by Whyte-Melville, Walford, and Thackeray. But Mark and William get more work than all the rest.

Ola not having turned up, there could be no stalking, so the beautiful morning was wasted. The Skipper got so angry about it that he said he would go in his canoe to find the absentee, and take at the same time a lot of our surplus fish for the people at Gjendesheim.

Leaving the tent on its grassy sunlit lawn he walked down to the edge of the great lake, and turning over the smaller of the two canoes, which were lying bottom uppermost, launched her and got in with rod and fishing bag, and pushed off into the deep. Opposite to the place where the canoes were drawn up, and apparently only a hundred yards distant though really more than a mile away, were the snow-capped mountain steeps that rise almost perpendicularly from two to three thousand feet out of the lake; and for these he made, gradually becoming a mere twinkling speck till he faded out of sight from the tent. The lake was as smooth as glass, only occasionally rippled as some monarch of the deep, excited for once in his life by some specially fascinating fly, condescended to make a rush for it instead of the gentle suck by which he usually took his food, and the Skipper paddled leisurely along within twenty yards of the rocks, with his rod bending over the stern, and trailing behind a couple of flies in the hope of catching a trout without the trouble of angling for him.

It is very pleasant to be alone once in a way in this over-crowded world. Not alone as it is possible to be in England, but absolutely alone, with no living thing near except the trout, the insects, and one's image in the water. Oh, blessed Norway! when we get back to the turmoils, troubles, and pleasures of a London season how we shall long for you! There is only one word to express this existence, and that is Freedom—freedom from care, freedom from resistance, and from the struggle for life. What a country! where civilised man can relapse as much as seems good to him into his natural state, and retrograde a hundred generations into his primeval condition.

But we forget that the Skipper is coasting up towards Gjendesheim in search of the miscreant Ola.

He proceeded for a couple of hours, catching a few fish now and then, but presently, as midday approached, the sun became too hot to be pleasant, the fish would not move, and the Skipper began to get impatient and annoyed at not meeting Ola. After a while a black speck with two flashing arms appeared rounding a promontory; this was Ola in the boat. The Skipper was boiling with rage under the influence of various incentives as he approached. Ola, like most Norwegians, was calm, placid, and utterly unconscious of the flight of time and the shortness of life. The Skipper had been primed to exploding point by his two friends before starting, and as he had now paddled five miles from home without meeting the adversary, he was, to put it mildly, 'indignant.' So, when he found Ola smoking serenely, and sculling along as though his brief span were going to stretch through the unending cycles of eternity, he gave way to the most horrible outbreak of temper in English, which must have lasted four or five minutes, and then telling the caitiff in Norwegian to take the fish to Gjendesheim and return to camp by five o'clock whatever the weather might be, he turned and left that hardy Norseman open-mouthed and bewildered, looking as though he had seen the Strømkarl, or had had an interview with his mother-in-law.

Then a great wind arose, and blew against the Skipper all the way home, but he arrived in the most beatific frame of mind in spite of it; the relief of the storm of temper and bad language had been so great to him, that he was filled with a

blessed joy. He said it was the most invigorating and refreshing pastime he ever indulged in, for Ola could not understand a word of it, and therefore no remorse could follow the outburst, not a thoughtless expression or hasty word could go home to his heart and there rankle, to recoil on some future occasion, but the whole vial of pent-up wrath could be emptied on its object without fear of retribution.

The explosion must have been something very fine to enable the Skipper to make light of the head-wind, for a wind on Gjendin is not to be scoffed at in any boat, and least of all in a cockle-shell of a canoe. The mountains are so high and steep that the lake lies as it were in a trench, and any wind always draws straight up or down the length, and soon gets a big sea up. All the Norwegians we have seen say it is the height of madness to go on Gjendin at all in such boats, the sudden squalls are so dangerous; and neither of our men can be persuaded to go a yard in them.

CHAPTER XXII.

MEMURUDALEN.

Sunday, August 22.—We spent the morning in quiet Sunday fashion, chiefly in lying under the shade of an awning made with rugs which we call the 'sycamine tree,' and eating wimberries and cream. Besides this we perpetrated a great deal of high art; every one was seized with the desire of sketching the camp, and so we sat around on pinnacles like so many pelicans, libelling the unfortunate place from every position whence it could be seen.

It is looking very comfortable just now. The tent itself is pitched in an angle of a steep little cliff which effectually protects it from cold winds at one side and the back, and at the other side we have put up a thick fence of birch branches to temper the storm to the sleeping-tent. We find it very convenient to have the two compartments: the inner one is only used for sleeping in, and always immediately after reveillé is plunged in an apparently hopeless confusion of rugs, sheepskins, mattresses, and boots, with here and there a book or a hat protruding (to use the Skipper's beautiful simile) like brickbats in a dust-heap. After breakfast all the bedding is dragged out to be aired on the rocks, and the tent generally tidied.

But the outer tent is always a picture of order and neatness, for here we keep our stores, boxes of flour and biscuits, cartridges, cooking utensils, tools, whisky, and potatoes. One of the boxes was made specially under Esau's directions to be used as a table: the top and bottom are both hinged, and so when the box is put on its front and these two lids opened it makes a very good large table; the lids are held up by a batten screwed underneath them, and for greater security we have added two legs. But at present the weather is so pleasant that we always feed outside, a few yards from the tent and nearer to the oven.

On the extreme left, as the penny showman says, you will observe one of the meat safes, the other one 'thou canst not see, because it's not in sight,' being close to the back of the tent. Also behind the tent may be faintly seen the mustard and cress garden, always covered with a sheet by day to save it from the heat of the sun, and with the same sheet by night, to guard it from the cold, so that the poor thing never gets any light, and does not flourish very exceedingly. None of the mustard seeds have as yet grown up as big as the one in the parable, but when one does we mean to make a lot of salad out of it, enough for all the camp.

Above the middle of the outer tent are three things which look like lightning conductors, but are only our rods, which are always stuck in the ground there when not in use. At their foot under the rock is the egg larder, neatly constructed of stones and turf, with a wooden lid; and hanging from the cliff hard by is a very pretty and curious spider's nest made of paper, like a miniature wasp-nest, about two inches in diameter.

High up in the centre is 'the meteor flag of England' engaged in its customary occupation of 'yet terrific burning,' there being absolutely no Dutch Boers here. Underneath its shelter are many forked poles with cross-bars, all made from the birch with which the valley abounds just here, and on which clothing of some sort is always hanging out to dry; so that the place looks like a laundry-ground, and deceives even the ravens, which come down in swarms from the mountains in search of maids' noses to devour. In the midst of these poles may be seen the oven, with its flue reaching half-way up the hill, and its two openings, the lower one for fuel, the upper for food.

Right in front of the tent is the fireplace, a long trench in the ground, faced with stones of such a size and shape that they form apertures suitable for our numerous pans; and simmering by the fire is the perennial soup. Nearer to the front is the wood pile, and nearer still the board on which the cooking things are placed after washing up. In front again of this is the little stream which supplies us with water, now rapidly beginning to fail under the influence of the long drought: it may be noticed that the engineers have changed

its course in several places for greater convenience in getting water, and to give more room on the camp side.

The foreground is a mass of juniper, wimberries, skintukt, crowberries, and rocks, and then comes about thirty yards from the tent the Memurua torrent, all thick and milky from the glacier, cold as Christmas, fishless, uninteresting, not drinkable, only useful as a refrigerator for milk, and only agreeable to look upon from a distance, but faithfully keeping up the unceasing roar that is customary among such torrents. This river makes the waters of the lake too cold to bathe in and too cheerless for fish to abide in near our camp, but it does not come into the picture, partly because it runs in a ravine, but more because it was right behind the artist.

The lake itself is to the extreme right, with unclimbable snow-capped rocky mountains forming the opposite coast.

To-day we dined at 4 P.M. in order to get an uninterrupted evening's fishing, but the experiment was not a success and will not be repeated, for it spoilt the dinner and we caught no fish.

On returning to camp at night rather cold, very cross, and exceedingly hungry, we agreed that the best antidote for these dangerous symptoms would be hot soup, so John put the pot on the fire, while the Skipper and Esau were attending to the tent and domestic duties.

Soon the caldron was heated and brought into the tent, and the eager crowd drew near with cups and spoons, and one lifted the lid, while another plunged his cup into the steaming savoury mess. And then arose a great cry of horror and desolation, and the sleeping valley rang with the wail of men in despair, for John had put the wrong pot on the fire, and we had been presented with boiling dirty water in which the dinner-things had been washed up; while all the time the soup pot was quiet, untouched, and cold in the corner of the tent where it is kept.

But three hungry men are not to be balked of a meal on which their hearts are set by any trifle like this, so we all commenced with a will to stoke that fire up and put that other pot on, and we got our soup and were snugly packed in bed long before the gentle August moon had sunk to rest behind the sheltering mountain tops.

The skipper, by the way, is very much exasperated with this same moon just now. He says she is a fraud, for this morning when we got up, there she was high in the heavens. 'What right,' he wants to know, 'has this moon—any moon in fact—to be up there blinking away in the middle of the day when we have plenty of sun to light us? forward, dissipated thing! and then probably after this week we shall have ever so many nights without any moon at all, and all the earth left in total darkness to take care of itself; while here we are to-day with an absurdly round moon at one end of this comparatively diminutive valley, and a most extravagantly blazing sun at the other.' The whole thing is ridiculous, he says, and it must be confessed that there is some justice in his complaint; though no doubt there could be a good deal said on the other side.

August 23.—While Esau went out after deer the other two crawled up the mountain and over to Rus Vand to fish, and had a good day. Two of the Skipper's fish were three pounds each, but, like most of the biggest fish, not in that beautiful condition which the smaller ones always show. The Skipper is sure that the old worn-out fish creep up to the stony shallows at the western end of the lake to die in a sunny spot, just as we men creep away in our old age to Bath, Cheltenham, Cannes, or Algiers, to breathe our last in a warm place, thereby taking one step in the direction of the proverbial future.

Esau arrived in camp about half-past seven quite exhausted, and followed by Ola, also dead beat, and again bearing the heads and skins of two deer, a buck and a doe. He was hailed with fervent joy and many congratulations: it is certainly great luck to fall in with deer on two stalking days in succession, for they are by no means numerous here this year. Dinner was served in a marvellously short time.

MENU.—August 23.

Poisson.

Truite à la Fried in Butter.

Entrées.

Kari of Reindeer Tongue

Rôts.

The Boss Pie

Gibier.

Ryper à la Spitchcock.

Entremets.

Jam. Wimberrytart. Marmalade.

Potage.

Could not eat any.

Then came Esau's romance.

'We walked up the Memurua to the great glacier, and then skirted its south side. We found many fresh tracks, and about two o'clock, when we were seven miles from home, Ola spied three deer chewing stones about three-quarters of a mile away. The wind was just in the right direction to allow us to approach them, and they were in capital ground for stalking, full of little hollows and slopes. But there was a serious drawback: on one side was a lake, on the other an impassable precipice; and before we could get into a place out of their sight we should be obliged to cross a narrow strip of ground in full view of them, though perhaps half a mile from them. We sat down and had our lunch, and waited an hour watching for them to lie down, and at last they did so; then we determined to risk the passage of the dangerous strip, and by crawling like serpents and aided by luck got across without the deer seeing us. Then we had to creep along the side of a scandalous precipice for the next half-mile, in no danger of being seen, but with our hearts constantly in our mouths, as, despite our care, some stone was dislodged and went clattering down the rocks, sounding to my strained ears as if it must disturb every living thing within a mile. Very slow and difficult was our progress, occasionally dangerous, but at last we arrived at a spot 200 yards from the deer, which were still lying down, and pronounced by Ola to be a buck and two does.

'This was a very awkward place to shoot from, and I thought I could see my way to a better one much nearer, so tried it and found it was just possible, and after about a quarter of an hour's worming, I arrived at a place only 100 yards from them. From this I could see both the does well, but only the head of the buck, and so had to lie there an hour waiting for him to get up. Both the does did so twice, offering beautiful shots, but he would not move, and they lay down again. I dared not whistle to make him jump up, for fear the does might possibly be in the way at the moment. So there I lay, miserably uncomfortable, with cramp in every muscle; and at last I tried to crawl to another stone about five yards away, from which I thought I could see to shoot at the buck. When I got to it and peered cautiously over, I was horrified

to see the deer some distance away, and running as hard as they could towards a small glacier which was close to them.

'Of course I instantly lost my head, and jumping up fired at the buck without much aim, and missed him. Then I recovered my senses and made a careful shot at the last doe, knocking her over like a rabbit. The other two were just then out of sight in a hollow, but they appeared directly going up the hill on the snow at a great speed; and getting a broadside shot at the buck I broke his shoulder; after this he went slowly, but still kept on up the hill, and when he was about three hundred yards away I fired two more shots, one of which hit him in the ribs, and the other cut one of his horns off. Then he gave up trying to mount the hill, and turned down towards the lake out of my sight. I ran as hard as I could across the shoulder of the glacier, and saw him standing down below me among the rocks close to the water, and sitting down I fired another shot which killed him.

'This is not a creditable performance in the shooting line; but my solid bullets have a good deal to do with the matter: either of the first two shots would have stopped him at once if fired from an express with hollow-pointed bullets.

'The doe is a barren one with a beautiful skin, and very fat, and the buck is the best we have killed at present this year, a four-year-old, what Ola calls a "litt stor bock" (little big buck), which I suppose is the next best thing to the mythical "meget stor bock," whose footprints we are always seeing, but who carefully absenteth himself whensoever the jovial hunter goeth forth to pursue him.

'We saw a great deal of fresh spoor to-day, so that we may hope the deer are beginning to come to our part of the country: perhaps the poor things have been very much bullied in other places. Anyhow they won't find any better country in Norway than where we went to-day; and the scenery there is glorious.'

Esau was so tired that he fell asleep once in the midst of his exciting narrative, and as dinner was very late we all turned in almost as soon as it was finished.

CHAPTER XXIII.

A PICNIC.

August 24.—There is a brood of ryper on the brow of the mountain above our camp, which we always put up when we walk over Glopit armed with rods, but never when we take a gun. There were originally eight of them, but one has succumbed to a merlin which hunts up there; and they are remarkably tame, so that when we put them up we throw stones at them, and fully expect to kill them by that means, but somehow they have escaped with their lives until now. This conduct has become unbearable, and we have sworn 'this day that brood shall die;' so the first thing after breakfast Esau and the Skipper toiled up the mountain with pockets full of cartridges and guns ready for the slaughter of the innocents. It takes just three-quarters of an hour to get to the top; and after reaching it we tramped over some millions of acres in search of that brood, and of course it never obtruded itself on the scene. Finally the Skipper went home in disgust, remarking that 'he wished every ryper in Norway was at the bottom of Gjendin;' while Esau said 'he would stay up there a month or two and find those birds if they were anywhere on our sheet of the Ordnance map.'

The Skipper had hardly walked 200 yards towards camp before he trod on the old cock, who got up observing kek! kek! kekkekkek*kek*, kurrack: kur*rack*; kurrack, krackrackackckkkkk! in an extremely indignant tone of voice, and the rest of the family immediately followed him, astonishing the Skipper so much that he missed the lot; and though we marked them down quite near we could not persuade any of them to risk their lives in flight again.

The language used on this occasion scorched the herbage off so large a patch of ground, that John down below thought that Glopit had suddenly commenced a volcanic eruption.

After lunch we all manned Esau's canoe, which is the largest, because he is the smallest man; and set off down the lake to Leirungsø, the place where the professor's hut is built at the edge of the waterfall which runs out of a small lake there (not the real Leirung's Vand, which is further to the east).

The Skipper had noticed a remarkably fine bed of moltebær there, which we expected to be just about ripe now, and so we had determined to picnic (!) there, forsooth, as if our life were not one perpetual and perennial picnic.

We beguiled the journey home by songs and accompaniments by the following celebrated artists: Messrs. John, Skipper, and Esau. Among other songs was an original composition by John—air 'Bonnie Dundee'—

ODE TO THE LAST POT OF MARMALADE.

To the fishers of Gjendin the bold Skipper spoke:
'There is one two-pound pot that as yet is unbroke;[1]
So rouse ye, my gallant, and after our tea
Let us "go for" our Keiller's[2] own Bonnie Dundee.'

(Chorus,) Come! up with the Smör![3] Come! out with the Brod,[4]
We'll have one more Spise[5] that's fit for god;
Come, whip off the paper and let it gae free,
And we'll wade into Keillers own Bonnie Dundee.

You may talk of your molte[6] with sugar and milk,
Your blueberry pasties, and jam of that ilk;
They are all very well in the wilds, don't you see?
But they can't hold a candle to Bonnie Dundee.
Chorus as before.

Oh! the pies they were good, and the oven baked true,
With its door of green sod, and its sinuous flue.
Oh! the curry was toothsome as curry can be,
But where is the equal of Bonnie Dundee?
Chorus again, gentlemen.

There are ryper on Glopit[7] as fleet as the wind,
And the Stor[8] Bock roams on the Skagastolstind;
There are trout, teal, and woodcock, a sight for to see,
But what meal can be perfect without our Dundee?
Chorus, if you please.

Pandecāgos[9] are tasty, and omelettes are good;
Our eggs, though antique, not unsuited for food;
You can always be sure of at least one in three,
But blue mould cannot ruin our Bonnie Dundee.

Chorus, only more so.

Take[10] my soup, though 'tis luscious my öl,[11] though 'tis rare,
My whisky, though scanty, beyond all compare;
Take my baccy, take all that is dearest to me,
But leave me one spoonful of Bonnie Dundee

Chorus, ad lib.

Esau supplied an encore verse:—

It has made our lot brighter, and helped us to bear
Our troubles, the rain, mist, and cold northern air;
And the Gjende fly,[12] green fly,[13] bug,[14] skeeter,[15] and flea,
We should ne'er have *done Deeing* them but for Dundee.

Chorus (of big, big D's).

NOTES ON THE ABOVE COMPOSITION.

[1] 'Unbroke.' This is bold poetic imagery, meaning unopened. Breakages were unknown during our expedition, and long experience justifies us in assuring the world that breaking the pot, though an effectual way of getting at the marmalade, is not a satisfactory method. It will be found much better to remove the bladder at the top. This may be depended on.

[2] Need we explain that 'Keiller's own Bonnie Dundee' alludes to the marmalade made by the great and good man? No, a thousand times no!

[3] 'Smör,' Norwegian butter, pronounced Smoeurr—and it tasted like this, too.

[4] 'Brod,' bread. The word does not rhyme to god, being pronounced something like Broat, but it looks as if it rhymed.

[5] 'Spise,' a meal, pronounced Speessa.

[6] 'Molte,' cloudberry, pronounced Moulta.

[7] 'Glopit,' the mountain between Gjendin and Rus Vand.

[8] 'Stor,' big, pronounced Stora before a consonant.

[9] 'Pandecāgos,' pancakes.

[10] 'Take.' This word is only used by poetic licence, and must not be construed literally. When we attempted to 'take' John's whisky on our return to camp, there was a good deal of ill-feeling engendered, and he said that no one but himself understood the subtleties of æsthetic metaphor.

[11] 'Öl,' the ale of the country, 'rare' both in quality and, alas! in quantity.

[12] 'Gjende fly,' a fly peculiar to this lake, of which more anon.

[13] 'Green fly,' a charming creature like a large grey blue-bottle with green eyes: it bites a portion of flesh sufficient for its wants, and then goes away to eat it.

[14] 'Bug,' Again poetic licence. *Cimex lectularius* has not been encountered during our stay in Norway this time; nevertheless he is not unknown in the country, as the sojourners in one of the Lillehammer hotels, *not* the Victoria, can testify.

[15] 'Skeeter.' The mosquito is a mournful and disgraceful fact; and so are the sand-fly, stomoxys, and the flea. Memurudalen is more free from insects than any place we have tried.

August 25.—Still the same glorious weather, rather too glorious for our purling rivulet, which has now dwindled away to a mere thread of water, while even the larger stream on the hill behind the tent, which we use for bathing, is showing a marked decrease in volume.

The Skipper and Ola went out stalking directly after breakfast, and Esau climbed up on to Bes Hø to shoot ryper. John went over to Rus Vand to fish, and had a pleasant day. He managed somehow to drop his native 'tolle kniv' into the lake, and of course immediately discovered that that knife was the most precious thing he possessed, in fact, the only thing he cared about in this world; though until it fell into the lake, he had regarded it with very unenthusiastic feelings—feelings of tolle-ration, the Skipper said. So he undressed and dived for it for a long time, and at last was lucky enough to recover it.

It would have been a pleasing sight to a spectator, if any

could have been present, to watch John playing at being a seal all by himself in Rus Vand, or standing on a rock poised on one leg like a heron, with his head sideways and keen eye piercing the cerulean wave. And it was good to see his proud bearing as he returned to camp with the 'tolle kniv' slung jauntily at his waist, and carrying over his shoulder the scaly spoil snatched from the vasty deep, as we used beautifully to word it in Latin verses—meaning the fish he had caught.

At 8 P.M. the Skipper had not returned, so we dined, and then sat round the fire wondering what could have happened to delay him; and as time went on and still he never came, we began to get very uneasy; there are so many dangers by which the reindeer hunter may be overtaken—avalanches, crevasses, fogs, snowdrifts, broken limbs, or getting lost. We could only hope that none of these had happened to the Skipper, and at eleven o'clock gave up any hopes of his return that night and turned in, there being then a very decided fog a short way up the Memurua valley.

CHAPTER XXIV.

THE SKIPPER'S RETURN.

August 26.—Lunch-time passed, and still the Skipper had not returned, so we decided that he must be defunct, and proceeded to write his epitaph, preparatory to organising a search expedition to bring in his remains.

Here is one touching little poem:

He was rather tall and terribly thin,
But remarkably roomy inside;
We put up these stones to cover his bones
Near the place where we think he died.

This is another:

IN MEMURUHAMEREN

(HILLS ROUND THE CAMP).

Our Skipper has gone, our great head cook,
  On a tour that e'en Cook won't find;
In a fissure he's surely taken his hook,
  Nor left any trace behind.

With a rod or pole he would fish for perch,
  Now a rod, pole, or perch of ground
Is more than he needs, and in vain we search,
  For his body will ne'er be found.

Now his angling is finished, though once every fin
  Which came within reach he'd attach;
He was really so clever at reeling them in,
  And his terms were to fish, 'nett catsh.'

On a lake or pond, or even a moat,
  He beamed wherever he went;
How cheerfully he would tar his boat!
  How gaily would pitch his tent!

After ryper or deer he would walk all day,
  From the top of a hill to the bottom;
And we feel it unpleasantly sad to say
  That the dear old Reaper's got him.

But we think it is time that this verse were done,
  Which to mournfully write we've tried
In memory o' our darlin' one,
Who in Memurudalen died.

While we were still lingering over these beautiful and appropriate sentiments, and deliberating as to whether they should be cut on a stone or only on wood, the corpse suddenly walked into the tent and announced that he wanted something to eat. We soon got over our natural disappointment at the waste of a good epitaph, and really welcomed him quite warmly, much more so when Ola appeared laden with the tit-bits of a reindeer buck. Then we set food before the Skipper, and after he had feasted he related unto us his story.

'I left camp yesterday morning determined to beard the savage untamed reindeer of the mountains in his lair, and soon came on very fresh tracks, which we followed for some time, and at each step seemed to get "hotter," as the children say, and the indications of deer being near got more and more encouraging. However, by one o'clock we had seen nothing, so sat down behind a little rocky eminence to have our "spise." Mine was a particularly good lunch, as I had spread some gravy from the "boss pie" on my slice of bread and butter, and this with the icy cold snow-water was very grateful after a four hours' walk uphill under a scorching sun.

'Ola also seemed to devour his food with considerable relish. So we had been sitting there some time, happily silent, as we cannot talk each other's tongue, and I was just preparing to move on, and putting my knife back in its sheath, when we heard a slight snort quite close to us.

'Ola immediately peeped cautiously over an adjacent stone; then he pushed my rifle into my hand and whispering the magic word "Reins," pointed to another stone a few yards away, whither he wished me to crawl. To unsling my cartridge-bag lest it should jingle, and creep to that stone, was what the novelists call the work of a moment: then I raised my head *va-a-ry* gingerly, and saw forty yards away a single four-year-old buck standing broadside to me with his head in the air, sniffing suspiciously, and his whole attitude denoting uncertainty and caution. This buck, as we found out afterwards from the spoor, had walked up to within ten yards of us as we sat at lunch; then he must have either heard me or

smelt Ola, probably the latter, for Ola seldom washes his hands, never his blood-stained hunting coat; and when I encountered his gaze he had evidently just decided that this was not a good place for reindeer to be about in. This was an excellent frame of mind on his part, but he arrived at it a couple of seconds too late: my rifle was levelled, and the shot hit him just above the heart. At that distance the express bullet smashed a portion of him about as big as a hat, so that he rolled over stone dead, and had no time for lingering glances or last words. Half an hour more, and he was skinned, gralloched, put in a hole and buried under a heap of stones, to remain there until we need his flesh and send the horse to bring him home. Then we built a little cairn to mark his resting-place for future use, and wandered on in search of the rest of his party.'

'Very soon we came on the tracks of four other deer, one of them only a calf, but although we followed the spoor all the afternoon we never came up with them: probably they were near enough to hear my shot when I fired, and at once betook themselves to remote regions.

'It had got so late before we gave up the search, and we were such a long way from home, that we determined to go to Gjendebod, at the western end of the lake, hoping to get a boat there and return to Memurudalen by water. But on arriving there very tired, hot, and hungry, we found that the men had taken their boat down the lake, and would not return until to-day. This was a great blow, for it is quite impossible to walk along the shores of Gjendin, except, as John says, for a bird—and even it would have to fly all the way. Climbing up the mountain again was out of the question, as it is a seven hours' walk from Gjendebod to our camp, so there was nothing for it but sleeping there—a course which was very distasteful to me, as the food is bad, and I had no book with me, no tobacco, no hair-brush, and no fishing-rod.'

We celebrated the joyful reunion of loving hearts by a skaal, and so to bed, perfectly happy after the events of the day.

August 27.—We sent the men off this morning with the horse to bring in some of the meat now lying in the mountains, while we went by canoe to Gjendesheim to stay for a couple of days, as we cannot go stalking again till the already slain deer are brought home; the fish in the lake are not rising well after this long spell of fine weather, and with the exception of Esau's 'home coverts' there is no shooting for a fowling-piece at Memurudalen.

Very few tourists find their way to Gjendin, but the season for them is over, and we expected to have the place to ourselves; but how fallible is human prescience! To our astonishment the sportsmen from Rus Vand had already occupied the greater part of the house, having abandoned their own hut

for the same reasons which had led us to forsake our camp, and here they were, armed to the teeth with rods and guns.

This seemed unlucky, and although we were outwardly glad to see them, at heart we could not help feeling how inconsiderate it was of them to come and shoot the fjeld and fish the river just when we wanted to do all that ourselves. No doubt they harboured precisely the same feelings towards us.

However, we had dinner together, and introduced the 'boss pie,' now rapidly disappearing, to the notice of our Norwegian friends, and as the meal advanced a feeling of genial contentment crept over us, which seemed to influence all our senses; we began to talk over sport and compare our experiences in various countries and in pursuit of various animals: some of us were good listeners, others fond of talking but all animated by a love for the same occupation, so that when at length one of the enemy handed round the best of cigars, even the Skipper became so mellow and pleasant that before going to bed we arranged for a joint shoot after ryper to-morrow; and said 'Good night,' feeling that it was quite fortunate that we had all come to Gjendesheim on the same day.

CHAPTER XXV.

THE GJENDE FLY.

August 28.—The river, Gjendinoset as it is called, just in front of the rest-house, is a wonderful piece of water; there are about 150 yards of rapid in which the fish lie, then comes a fall, and below that there are nothing at present but small fish, though the big ones will soon begin to drop down lower for spawning. Consequently we all fish in the first 150 yards, and to-day between 50 and 60 lbs. weight has been taken out, the same quantity yesterday, and probably for some days before; and the fishing will be even better a few days later, for the Gjende fly is beginning to hatch, and as long as he lasts the fish will rise well.

We have heard so much of this fly that we had been expecting something rather gorgeous, a monster dragon-fly, or at least a second-rate butterfly, or a decent imitation of a stag-beetle; and we have been looking up gaudy Scotch and Canadian salmon flies, which we hoped might be passable substitutes; but, alas for the vain hopes of foolish man! the Gjende fly has come, and he is only a wretched little black beast like a very small, unenterprising, common or garden house-fly of Great Britain. He cannot fly decently; he is apparently devoid of sense; he has no moral, physical, or intellectual attributes for which a human being can learn to respect or love him; but—he *can* CRAWL. If he alights on the water it never occurs to him to rise again, and he allows the trout, mad with the excitement of a fortnight's prospective gluttony, to scoop him down their capacious throats by companies. If he enters your mouth, which he does with a numerous retinue every time you open it, retreat from that untenable position is the very last thing he would think of; and with what may be a gleam of momentary intelligence he seems desirous of still further increasing his knowledge of the rest of your interior arrangements.

With characteristic obstinacy, unmindful of the teachings of logic, he invariable acts on the fallacious maxim that 'an ink-bottle cannot be so full that there is not room for just one more Gjende fly.' The whole of the river here at the end of the lake, and for thirty yards on each side, is now pervaded by this noisome creature; the water looks as if it were covered with a mixture of soot and tar, the rocks are black and slippery with him, and the atmosphere is charged with him, so that the landscape dimly seen through the cloud looks as it if were dancing.

If any one stuck up a rod near the river, in two minutes it looked like a black fir pole with a bunch on the top: and John, who is a man of great entomological knowledge, spent some time in studying this phenomenon. He reported that the flies crawled up for fun, intending to jump off the top ring, but when they got up it was so much higher than they expected that they were all afraid to try, and those at the bottom and halfway up kept jeering at the top ones and calling them names, and jostling them so much that they could not crawl down again. He also said that the swarm in the air was so dense that he wrote his name in it with his finger, and it remained visible for nearly a minute.

Probably it is difficult for a man to speak the exact truth with his mouth full of (*f*)lies.

When it was too dark to fish we sat round the fire and heard a good deal about the various winter sports of Norway, capercailzie stalking, bear hunting, elk and reindeer shooting, and running on skier, the snowshoes of the country, which are very different from the well-known Canadian shoes, being made of wood, from six to twelve feet long, four inches wide in front, three behind, about an inch and a half thick where the foot rests, thinner at each end, and turned up and pointed in front. Every district has its own peculiar shape; about here the right shoe is made six feet long, the left one ten or eleven feet, it being more easy to turn if one is shorter than the other: some are made of pine, some of birch, and occasionally oak. The men of the Thellemarken are the most skilful runners, but it is now quite a fashionable amusement in Christiania during the winter, just as skating is in England.

Sunday, August 29.—Our Norwegian friends departed for the happy hunting-grounds of Rus Vand this morning, but before doing so they most kindly offered us the hut there any time after this week, at the end of which they are going south. We can hardly expect the present glorious weather, which has now lasted for three weeks, to go on for ever; and when the change comes, a tent will no longer be the abode of comfort and luxury that we at present find it, so that the offer of the hut is most opportune for us.

We parted with great regret from people who have been so kind and hospitable, and many were the expressions of good-will and protestations of eternal friendship, as we shall not see them again till we pass through Christiania on our return home.

That return home has caused the Skipper hours of anxious thought already: there is to be a wedding in England about the ending of next month, at which, although it is not his own, his presence is urgently needed. He knows he ought to go, but hates to leave this blissful life just when the best stalking is beginning; consequently he devotes much time every day to the consideration of the subject, torn by doubts, tortured by terrible misgivings, and harassed by indecision.

The ponies of Norway are wonderfully docile and clever; these qualities were well shown to-day in a black one belonging to Jens which came to take F——'s baggage over the mountain to Rus Vand. This pony was brought down near the door of the rest-house, and left standing there without any fastening or any one to look after him. The things were not ready, so he waited about two hours, occasionally wiping off the Gjende flies with his tail when their weight became insupportable, but otherwise never moving. The busy world (consisting of Andreas and Ragnild) pursued their usual avocations around him, goats ran against him, and insects climbed over him, but there he stood placid and motionless as a wooden rocking-horse. At last the baggage was ready, and they brought it out and piled it on his back until we feared he would break, and then Jens turned his head in the direction of Rus Vand, and gave him a gentle push to start him; and he went slowly off up the mountain, choosing the best way for himself, for no one went with him; in fact, Jens did not follow him for about half an hour, but no doubt he was found at the right place in the end.

The whole performance reminded one of a clockwork toy, and John remarked as we stood and watched him out of sight over the pass, 'Now, that's what I call a well-trained pony.'

During our stay here we had the pleasure of forming the acquaintance of an elk-dog. This animal is taken out in a kind of harness to which a rope is fastened, the other end of the rope being attached to the hunter's belt; and his legitimate occupation is finding elk in a forest by scent, and denoting their presence by his behaviour before the hunter gets within range of the elk's eyes, ears, or nose. Mr. Thomas brought him up here hoping to find reindeer with him in the same manner, as he had been unable to get a Finmarker[1]) broken to reindeer; but the experiment has not been successful, for the dog has been so carefully trained to elk, that he exhibits a large and lofty contempt for so pusillanimous a creature as a reindeer, and will not confess that he has discovered the existence of such a thing at all.

But in addition to the fact that he finds no deer, he is a good deal of trouble from the fastidiousness of his appetite. It appears that he is accustomed to feed on dogs, and when he cannot get dogs he can rough it very well for a short time on boys or any other plain fare; but up here, where dogs are few and boys are extinct, he is having a very poor time of it. The last place where he had a really square meal was at Skjæggestad, on the journey up, where he was lucky enough to get a whole dog and some portions of boy; since then he has only had limbs snatched off adventurous observers, and altogether seems to be pining for want of proper nourishment. He is about the height of a collie, but with an enormous chest and limbs, a head something like an Esquimaux, a wiry reddish yellow coat, and a most unkindly expression of countenance. In the absence of sufficient flesh food he appears to be developing a liking for man-diet, so we did not remain long in his society, for which indeed we only craved after we had perceived through a chink in the door of his dwelling that he was moored to a beam by a kind of anchor chain. We have often heard that there is a certain amount of danger in the pursuit of the elk; if the hunter is always accompanied by a dog of this kind we can easily understand it. However, he was a very interesting animal, and if we had a National School at Memurudalen we should certainly have tried to buy him,

[1]) Finmarker is the kind of dog usually employed for finding reindeer the name being derived from the district of which it is a native.

as there is any amount of room for *débris* there. What a boon he would be in some of the thickly populated districts of England!

In the afternoon we paddled leisurely back to our camp and found it looking prettier than ever, but, alas! our little stream had ceased to run. However, there is another one not more than forty yards away, so we shall not be much troubled by its loss.

August 30.—The most prominent object in looking towards the lake from our camp is a curious pyramidal mound, about thirty feet high, close to the water's edge. It is so regular in shape that we have devoted many hours of cogitation and argument to the discovery of its history.

John (who is a man of considerable archæological fame) maintains that it is a funeral barrow in which some ancient Viking was buried, and he wants us to give up our cartridges for the purpose of constructing a mine and blasting him out: we have vainly represented to him that it cannot be a Viking's tomb, because there is absolutely nothing to Vike up here.

The Skipper says it is a glacial moraine, 'any donkey can see that at a glance;' and Esau holds to the opinion that it is an artificial mound put up for ancient regiments of Gjendin yeomen and Memurudalen militia to practise archery at. Possibly none of these theories give the correct solution; but whatever its origin, it makes a capital rifle butt for our occasional shooting. Esau was heard to irreverently remark, as he aimed at it with the Skipper's rifle, 'he guessed an express bullet would rouse old Jarl Hakon out of that,' but nothing particular followed.

CHAPTER XXVI.

DISASTER.

August 31.—We have got quite tired of writing 'Another beautiful day,' and in future shall bring notebooks to Norway with these words ready-printed at the top of each page.

The Skipper paddled away to Gjendebod, to bring home the deerskin which he had left there to dry. He returned with a splendid bag of the best trout that ever came out of Gjendin, and that means the best in the world; but he was in a state of great indignation because he had been charged 5*s.* 6*d.* for beds, dinners, and breakfasts for himself and Ola when they stayed there a few nights ago. This is the result of living in a cheap country for two months; to the ordinary Englishman it would not appear an exorbitant hotel bill, especially when the hotel (!) is fifty miles from a town, and only open for two months in the year.

Just at bedtime Esau crawled into the tent saying that he had strained his back in lifting a stone; he was in such pain that he could hardly stand, and was white and shivering. We undressed him and put him to bed, and then produced the liniment from the 'medicine chest,' by which name we dignify the cigar-box which contains our little stock of drugs. Then John spent an hour viciously rubbing remedies into his victim's back, as one rubs oil into a bat, so that Esau presently groaned out, 'Thanks, John, I think that will do, I feel a great deal better now;' and certainly he did seem to experience a kind of relief as soon as the rubbing stopped. After this we turned in.

September 1.—Esau spent a sleepless night, and this morning could not move. Thereupon John nobly closed with him for another half-hour's rubbing, which had a decided effect, and after giving him some breakfast we carried him out and made a comfortable bed for him under the Sycamine tree, and there left him with the library and all his belongings in easy reach.

After lunch, John accomplished what has long been his great desire, the ascent of the sugar-loaf mountain across the Memurua; and after boiling a thermometer at the topmost peak, burying a pocket handkerchief (thoughtfully borrowed from Esau, who was too unwell to refuse him anything), and 'carving his name on the Newgate Stone with his Tollekniv fine tra la,' he returned in raptures about the view and overcome with sublime and poetical emotions, which did not subside until he had poured forth his soul to his two friends at dinner.

The Skipper stalked without success, though he found the tracks of a good herd that had only just passed over the ground. Though the day was so pleasant, he had not exactly enjoyed his walk, for he could not help being filled with gloomy forebodings about Esau; picturing to himself the difficulties that would arise in getting men to carry the invalid down to Christiania in a litter, with him yelling at every step. But behold, how untrustworthy a thing is imagination! when the Skipper arrived in camp, he was agreeably surprised to find the object of his solicitude sitting up and actually stirring the rice for the curry, so marvellous had been the effect of John's lubrication; assisted by the support to his back of a kind of splint composed of birch bark, a towel, and two straps.

September 2.—John ate new bread again for dinner yesterday, and the Skipper was aroused in the middle of the night by a claw reaching out from the adjoining bed, which clutched his pillow and rug and tried to drag them away; the whole of this being accompanied by blood-curdling groans and hideous yells. He became more peaceful after a short time, but the Skipper is now in mortal fear lest John should again suffer from indigestion, and again stretch out that gruesome claw, and grabbing him by the hair, drag him forth from the tent, and with demoniac shrieks stamp the life out of his frail body, while he makes the quiet valley re-echo to his triumphant mocking laughter. This, the Skipper asserts, would be only one step beyond his conduct of last night.

The latest scientific observations have caused us to reclassify the different altitudes thus:—First, the country of high cultivation and wild strawberries; above that the zone of uncleared pine forests and most of the berries; then the belt of stunted birches and black game; higher still, that of cows and goats; and above that, the country where reindeer flourish and snow lies all the year round. This takes us to the summit of all things earthly, and in this zone there is hardly any vegetation. Beyond it is the region of eagles, but in the present imcomplete state of human knowledge we have been content to explore this highest zone by letting our spirits soar aloft without our bodies.

Gjendin is just at the highest point of the stunted-birch belt, and when the wind gets into the N.W. the thermometer, without waiting to reflect, falls a great distance very hurriedly. John, having no sheepskin, suffers a good deal from the cold at night; and the haughtiness of his spirit is so far broken that he now sleeps in two pairs of trousers, three shirts, and a coat, besides all his rugs. A few short weeks ago he turned from us with an air of aristocratic nausea when we were getting into bed clothed in a single shirt and pair of trousers, donning for his part a linen night-shirt, an effeminacy previously unheard of in camp life.

These things are changed now, and it is difficult to persuade him not to go to bed with his boots on; but it has to be prevented on account of the new bread.

The monotony of an uneventful day was only broken by the occasional rubbing of Esau's back, amidst the victim's agonised appeals for mercy, as he thinks it is rubbed away to the bone. However, the effect is magnificent, and he can now hobble about camp and be useful to a certain extent.

Menu.—September 2.

Vins.	Truite à l'Irlandais.	*Légumes.*
Onion Sauce.	Salmi of Ryper.	Crumpets.
	Woodcock à l'Oven.	
	Compote of Rice and Wimberries	

After dinner we dug a small hole in the floor of the outer tent, in which we placed a spadeful of redhot embers from the fire. This is a capital device for obtaining warmth in a tent, as there is no smoke, and the embers keep glowing for a very long time; possibly it might be dangerous in a very close-fitting tent, but ours is airy, not to say hurricany.

Round this fire we sat and talked and smoked until bedtime, hoping against hope for a few more days of sunshine; but when we turned in, the wind was howling and moaning along the hill-side in a very ominous and unpleasant manner.

CHAPTER XXVII.

A CHANGE.

September 3.—'Forty below Nero' was the probable position of the thermometer during the night. Esau declares that his back is quite well, but it is suspected that he only does this in order to avoid the administration of further remedies by John.

However, we consider this such a successful cure that we here give our recipe for strained backs to an expectant world, not as a sordid advertisement, but from pure philanthropic motives.

'Take the patient and place him on a grassy spot in the sun, and lubricate with oil; rub this in for three hours with the hand; seize his wrist and feel the pulse (if you can find it), displaying at the same time a large gold watch; look profound; mutter inwardly. Now shift him gently to a shaded position; and having lighted a fire to the windward, prepare and cook thereon fourteen or fifteen pancakes, and administer while hot (as a mixture, not a lotion). Take care that the aroma of each cooking pancake is wafted in the direction of the patient. Carry this principle throughout all his nourishment. Explain to him that deer abound in the neighbouring mountains; show him quantities of fresh-caught fish and newly killed ryper; ensure a week of fine weather, and if this do not cure him he must be a *malade imaginaire.*'

Notwithstanding the improvement, of course Esau was not fit to go stalking, and this and other reasons suddenly induced us to leave Memurudalen to-day for good, and go to Gjendesheim on our way to Rus Vand. So we made a last gigantic pie, packed up, lunched, and then pulled down the tent, which had been standing so long now on the same spot, and embarked everything on board our two canoes and the Gjendesheim boat, which had been lent to us. Then the whole fleet sailed from these hospitable shores 'neath a stormy sky, with cold wind and rain, and the towering heights of Memurutungen all wrapped in angry clouds, frowning blackly above us.

It was quite sad to leave the snug little corner where we

have spent such a happy, careless time, with all the comforts which we have added gradually to our temporary home; and the valley looked very desolate without the tent, the cheerful fire, and 'the meteor flag.'

Esau's last act was to fill two brass cartridge cases with water and hammer them firmly into each other; the air-tight boiler so formed he put into the fire under the oven, and after waiting a short time for the explosion, forgot all about it and went away without telling any one. Just then John arrived at the spot to see if there were any loose belongings lying about, and was horrified to observe the oven suddenly elevate itself into the air and disappear among the clouds with a loud report. His mind at once reverted to the happy life of a landlord in co. Limerick, but he soon realized the true state of affairs, and came down to the lake muttering something about 'tomdamfoolery,' a Norwegian word which expresses censure of the silly custom of practical joking.

What rare times all the birds and beasts of prey will have for the next few days in Memurudalen! only to be equalled by the early days of the Australian gold fever. Nuggets of inestimable value in the shape of heads, tails, and other portions of reindeer, ryper, duck, and trout—intermingled with other delicacies, such as potato skins, jam and marmalade pots, and whisky bottles—will from time to time be unearthed amidst shrieks of triumph. 'Claims' will be run up to a fabulous price, and many a battle royal will be fought in that happy valley where we have spent a month of peace. As we depart in mournful silence, brooding over the days that are no more, we see in fancy the numerous bright eyes which from lairs and eyries are watching our every move, their owners all ready to swoop down on our *débris* as soon as we have passed out of sight.

The lake was very rough, and we were quite afraid of being swamped and losing our baggage from the magnitude of the big little waves; but luckily the boat took our heaviest things, or we should not have been able to venture; and so the canoes, lightly loaded and with all sail set, rode gallantly o'er the foaming billows, and we all got safe to Gjendesheim. The cheery fire in the room with its bare wooden walls and benches, made a picture which seemed the perfection of comfort after the chilly tent and the freezing N.W. wind.

'It is the black north-wester
  That's makes brave Englishmen
Use very naughty words, and wish
  Themselves at home again.'

One of the party is always telling us that he intends to inflict on the British public a narration of our experiences on this expedition, and although he has not yet begun to collect materials for the work, we have begun to invent titles for the book that is to be. One is 'England, Canada, and Norway,' being a description of Englishmen travelling in Norway with Canadian canoes; and we think this title might induce schoolmasters to buy it, under the impression that it is a geographical treatise on those countries.

The Skipper proposed 'The Fool with the Fowling-piece, or Fishing and Flyblows.' John's title was 'Mems, from Memurudalen, or Jottings from the Jotunfjeld;' and Esau suggested 'Glopit, top it, and mop it,' alluding, he said, to the state of John's forehead whenever he arrived at the summit of that mountain; but the explanation was received with such a chorus of 'Oh! $\left\{\begin{array}{c}\text{drop}\\ \text{stop}\end{array}\right\}$ it!' from the others that he gave up the idea.

One notion is to make the book a collection of cooking recipes for camp life, and call it 'Grunts from a Gourmand in Gulbrandsdalen, or Paragraphs from the Pen of a Pig;' but we think we should promote a more active sale among respectable people if it were called 'Self-Improvement, or Lights thrown on Good Living.'

Another idea is that it might get a sale by appearing surreptitiously among the Christmas books for the young, and for that purpose we should use the names of our two henchmen Anglicised. 'Oola and Eva: a Tale for Girls,' could not fail to attract the favourable attention of parents and guardians.

Possibly it might create a greater sensation if it were introduced to the world as 'Julia and Pausanias: an Idyll.' It is very difficult to decide on a good name, but we are all agreed that the name once found, it will be perfectly easy to write the book afterwards.

September 4.—How soothing and pleasant it is, when we hear the storm and rain shrieking and beating outside, to reflect that there is a good solid roof over our heads, and that we shall not be roused in the night by the cry of 'All hands turn out to slack off guy-ropes!'

This morning the lake was so rough that we perceived that we had been very lucky to make our voyage yesterday; we certainly could not have attempted it to-day. The man from Gjendebod was here, and started for the other end of the lake with Andreas in the big boat about nine o'clock, but at two they came back dead beat and wet through, having been obliged to desist from their attempt before they had gone two miles, and they considered themselves lucky to have got back.

The appearance of the lake is wonderfully fine as the

white-capped breakers come rolling in, flinging the spray high up the face of the opposing cliffs, and dashing with an angry roar against the black rocks where they jut out into the deep part of the lake.

We shot all the afternoon with almost unvarying luck, hardly ever losing a bird; now getting four barrels into a large brood, now picking up a solitary old cock that had selfishly separated himself from his family, and selected a particularly advantageous feeding-ground for his own exclusive benefit, and at intervals having a little recreation afforded by our men, especially the professional buffoon, Ivar.

In one marshy bit of ground a pair of short-eared owls were incautious enough to fly up in front of Esau, and were promptly added to the bag; they were in beautiful plumage, which was luckily not injured by the shot, so we were much pleased at getting them. Then we went towards the river into the ground frequented by ducks, and got a little shooting there, and finished the day by walking round the shoulder of the lower fjeld about the time that the ryper were coming there to feed, and so back to Gjendesheim. Altogether the walk was most enjoyable, and as we returned and gazed over Gjendin, the contrasts of storm and sunshine, tumbled clouds and rough waters, and occasional glimpses of the highest mountains gleaming through rifts in the surrounding blackness as the bright sunbeams lighted up their peaks of snow, formed the most striking picture of wild and desolate grandeur that can be imagined.

Esau's shooting is remarkably unerring, and we feel so annoyed with him sometimes when he *won't* miss even a palpably difficult chance, that we were quite glad a few days ago when he took such a long shot that it strained his gun, and the Skipper exclaimed, 'Ah, I told you you would, I've been expecting it all along.'

John had an unstrung kind of day. Starting down the river to fish soon after breakfast, he became so engrossed in his sport that he forgot all about lunch, and did not return till dinner-time, when he walked abstractedly into the room where we were sitting, and pulled out his watch; then after studying it and making calculations for a short time he remarked slowly, 'I left here at six minutes past ten, and hanged if it isn't ten minutes past six now; my watch must have stopped.' Then he wandered off upstairs to his room, still ruminating over this extraordinary occurrence to his watch; but in his absence Ragnild had changed all his things into another cabin without telling him anything about it, so that

he found his old habitation swept and garnished, and began to think, like Clever Alice, 'This is none of I.' However, he got over this difficulty and came down to dinner, still looking a trifle abstracted, but with his usual appetite. Afterwards the Skipper paddled him across the river to fish, and when coming back, John upset the canoe and nearly drowned them both in the presence of Esau and every native in the district, who joined in mocking them in the Norwegian tongue from the bank.

Finally he informed us that during his wanderings he had composed a short poem, 'which,' said he, 'as you have not heard it, I will now proceed to recite.'

So we went to bed.

CHAPTER XXVIII.

RAPID-RUNNING.

Sunday, September 5.—To-day the Skipper and Esau determined to try to run the canoes down the river to Sjødals Lake, where we intend to leave them during our stay at Rus Vand.

All things being ready, the Skipper started about eleven o'clock on his perilous voyage, closely followed by Esau. The river is full of impracticable falls, some of them twenty or thirty feet high, but between these places there are splendid rapids, and the excitement of running them is delightfully fascinating. When we came to a bad fall we carried the canoes round, and enlisted the services of our two men to help us in this part of the performance. Ola did not like this at all, for carrying a canoe of 80 lbs. weight over very rough ground is hard work, and Ola loveth the fireside and the odour of roasting coffee better than hard work on the Sabbath.

Presently we came to a place which the Skipper wanted to run, but which Esau declared to be too dangerous; it was a very swift and rocky rapid, with two extremely sudden turns, the lower of which was only a few yards above a high fall. Esau only ran past the first turn, which was quite nervous work enough, and then got to shore and waited on the bank for the result of the Skipper's exploit.

Down he came at about fifteen miles an hour, took the first turn most successfully, and then, by some extraordinary strokes of his paddle, which no man living but himself could have performed, and aided by a species of miracle, he got round the second; but then an eddy caught the canoe, and she became unmanageable, so that instead of stopping in a little creek of quiet water as he intended, he came straight on at a terrific speed, and ran high and dry on a ledge of rock just above the fall, losing his paddle at the shock. Wonderful to relate, the canoe was not a bit injured, but the paddle whirled over the abyss and disappeared for ever; and the Skipper was pleased because he had not done the same.

We spent five hours in this kind of amusement, and enjoyed it almost more than anything else we have done. The constant danger of a smash or an upset, the sensation of speed, the delight of the sudden rush to the gliding dip over a fall, with the water roaring past a rock on each side; the big waves below the fall, which catch the canoe and toss it from one to another till you feel as if you must be thrown out; and the curious appearance that the hurrying foam-flecked waters all round present, combine to make Sunday rapid-running a very popular pursuit.

While we were doing the last bit above Sjødals Lake, our men, instigated no doubt by Ola the Lazy, seized the opportunity given by a long rapid to go home, and as we were pretty well tired out with our exertions, we left the canoes above the lowest fall and walked back to Gjendesheim. But we cannot recommend this river to future voyageurs; there are too many places that cannot be run; and we hear that we are regarded as decidedly mad for having attempted it.

Ola, our stalker, is a man whom we do not much admire. He is a big, handsome fellow, with a light beard and moustache, and rather a weak face; and his good qualities are extreme cleverness at almost any kind of work—carpentry, smith's work, needlework, and saddlery all seem to come alike to him—and as a deer-stalker he is first-rate, and never makes a mistake. But we fear that his profession at home is to be an independent gentleman, and he is very lazy, and nearly always

sulky. This sulkiness annoys us more than anything else, but we also get very angry with him for being afraid of everything. He is afraid to go in the canoes, and nothing has ever induced him to enter either of them. He is afraid of rowing against a wind, or going out stalking on two successive days, lest he should tire himself; and he is afraid of washing up plates and pans lest he should lose dignity; but it does not bore him to sit by and watch other people perform the operation.

September 7.—Andreas and Ragnild are making preparations for their departure, which takes place to-morrow; then Gjendesheim will be closed, the door fastened, the windows shuttered, and the place will be left to itself until next June. Very soon now Gjendin will be covered with ice and snow: most of the good folks in the sæters have already gone to the valleys for the winter.

We thought it would be more convenient for them if we took our departure to-day, so packed our goods on the pony and said 'Farvel' to Gjendesheim. Our last view of Gjendin, as we turned to look from the top of the pass, was just as it appeared when we first saw it—black, gloomy, and forbidding, with the cold north wind sweeping in a hurricane over its waters, and heavy rain-clouds hanging over its mountain shoulders, making a scene as awfully lonely and desolate as it is possible to depict.

Our first step at Besse Sæter was, as usual, to demand food; and John asked for a dish called 'Tuk melk,' which had been recommended to him as very Norwegian and very good. A woman at once went to fetch it from the other sæter, a quarter of a mile away, and presently brought it in a large wooden milktub about the size and shape of a sitz bath. How that poor woman carried it we know not; it occupied half the table, and was so scrupulously clean that we feared to touch it with our sordid hands.

John and Esau at last attacked it in the orthodox manner, which is to sit on opposite sides of the table, and to draw a line across the surface of the milk with a spoon before beginning, and then to 'eat fair' up to that line. It would have amused some of our friends at home if they could have seen these two young men of fashion at the moment when both of them were engaged with abnormally large wooden spoons, silently ladling down 'Tuk melk' out of a tub as big as a drawing-room table.

They reported that it was on the whole good; something like curds, but with a sourer taste, and it was much improved by sugar; but though they ate a large quantity of it, being men of great courage and determination, they could not persuade the Skipper to risk his life in experiments with untried articles of food. He, however, gave utterance to the following refined expression of his sentiments:—'I wouldn't touch that beastliness if you gave me fourteen pence a spoonful to swallow it.' No one offered the reward.

CHAPTER XXIX.

RUS VAND.

September 8.—This morning we crossed the fjeld to Rus Vand in a gale of wind. Waving a 'Farvel' to the kindly folk at Besse Sæter, we have a stiff climb up by the side of the torrent which comes gadareneing[1]) down from Bes Lake, high above our heads, and presently we stand on the open fjeld above the sæter. Below lie the green waters and birch-clad banks of Sjødals Lake; far away to the east the great fall and larger trees that mark the outlet of the lake; and still further, glimpses of lower Sjødals Lake, with its forests of pine, haunt of the black game and capercailzie. But we cannot stand long to look, for the side of a Norwegian mountain, though eminently suited to hurricanes, is extremely *un*suitable for human beings while the stormy winds do blow. En avant, Messieurs, en avant! and we fight our way across the flat top to the opposite brow. Here we must pause, though Æolus himself say nay. 'What a glorious sight!' Straight in front, the cloud-girt peak of Nautgardstind, all glistening white with newly fallen snow, but of him only the top can be seen; his middle is hidden by a never-ending rush of scudding clouds. Higher still and westward the jagged summits of Tyknings Hø and Memurutind, also pure white where the snow can lie, but with huge black lines and chasms where the steep rocky face stands up gaunt and repellent, so sheer that snow can never lodge; nearer the tremendous mass of Bes Hø frowns above us; and far below in front the Russen River winds its way through barren rocks and patches of willow, to warmer and more hospitable regions, leaving with a leap of

[1]) Gadareneing, *i. e.* rushing violently down a steep place.

joy the cold storm-rocked Rus Lake, which has been its cradle since its birth in the mighty glaciers around.

Such was the scene lying before us on the north side of the mountain, grand beyond description, perhaps the finest in Norway, but not exactly inviting to shivering hungry mortals, so not much time was spent on it. Down we went, with the wind worse than on the other side, howling past our ears and screeching in the gun-barrels, and at last arrived at the lake to find Jens hauling for his life at the boat, which though filled with water by the breakers, had fortunately not been battered to pieces on the rocky strand. He had left it dragged up on the beach out of the water, but the sea had increased so much in his absence, that if we had been a little later it would without doubt have been smashed.

However, we soon baled her out, and with Ola as Charon commenced the passage. Rusvasoset, as the outlet is called is not more than 60 yards across, but the waves had had seven miles of very open water to get up in, and they came rolling down to this end in a very alarming manner. With great difficulty we shoved off, and then with Ola sculling his hardest, and the Skipper keeping our head to wind, we at last got safe across with no mishap but the loss of Ola's hat and a thorough ducking for all of us.

Ola was very sorrowful about his hat, which was of pure Leghorn straw, double seamed, extra quality lining; and being further embellished with a black braid ribbon, it was a great source of pride to him; but we mocked when it flew away, and are inclined to bear its departure with equanimity, and hope it will be accepted as a propitiatory offering by the angry Lady of the Lake. All the things were at last safely housed, and we soon made ourselves comfortable in our new abode, which is luxury itself in this weather when compared with a tent.

There are two huts, one by the edge of the lake, the other about 20 yards away, and it is the latter which we occupy. We enter by a door about five feet high, invariably knocking our heads against the lintel and swearing as we do so. The first room is about nine feet square, with a narrow dresser under the solitary window on the left, and an iron cooking stove in the nearest corner to the right, the more remote one being tenanted by a bed. Round the room at various heights are shelves and hooks adorned by cooking utensils of all kinds, very kindly left for us by their worthy owners; two or three stools complete the furniture; and on the floor are to be seen carved the effigies of departed trout of fabulous weight, with dates and the initials of their captors. Passing on through a still smaller doorway we find ourselves in another room of the same size, but with three beds instead of one, and an open Norwegian fireplace; the same kind of pegs and shelves, and hooks for guns on the wall; more profile fishes, and walls covered with records in pencil of game killed by former inhabitants, with occasional amusing notes. This is our dining, drawing, and bed room; the other is only used as kitchen.

The men's hut near the water is also divided into two rooms: the outer and much larger compartment is used as a cellar, larder, and general store-room, and presents, to say the least of it, a somewhat untidy appearance, as bottles, barrels, and boards, a grindstone, reindeer bones, a saw, a side-saddle, and old nets are piled together without any attempt at order. The inner room is very small, about nine feet by four, and there our two men sleep; and there also is a large oven built of stone, and heated by a fire inside it. As we had no bread, we proceeded to bake, and our ignorance of the manners and customs of this oven caused the bread to have a terribly trying time of it; for we did not make it hot enough at the first attempt, and the bread was left lying on the top covered by a cloth for over an hour while the oven was being heated a second time.

All's well that ends well, and this batch of rolls turned out the very best that frail man ever tasted, and consequently at supper we ate enough bread and butter and jam to supply a school feast of the hungriest description.

While the Skipper and John attended to the loaves Esau looked after the fishes, and very soon got a nice dish of half-pounders in the river. As he came back something in the middle of the stream caught his eye. 'It is, yet it can't be—yes, by George, it is, Ola's hat!' wedged in between two rocks, and slightly out of shape, but with the double-seamed, extra quality lining uninjured, and the pure Leghorn straw in very fair condition. The effusion with which Ola received it was a sight to be seen, but no one else exhibited much enthusiasm.

An inventory of our remaining stores reveals the fact that we have heaps of everything except coffee and bacon, which can only last about a week longer. In view of this happy state of things the Skipper proposed to spend a week of wild and reckless profusion and sinful extravagance.

Esau at once pictured himself seated on a grassy slope giving way to Epicurean indulgence, surrounded by three untouched pots of jam, and eating from a fourth with a tablespoon; at his side a cup of tea blacker than ink, and flavoured with condensed milk thicker than cream, while he flipped lumps of sugar into the water instead of pebbles, and commanded Ola to sand the floor of the hut with pepper.

John suggested as an amendment that we should make some exception to show that we possess the power of self-denial. 'Let us,' said he, 'deny ourselves in some one thing. Not in luxuries, which are getting scarce; in that there would be no merit. No; rather let us exercise our virtue in respect of what we have in the greatest abundance, and thereby show a great and shining example to the world. Let us abstain entirely from water.' (He had ascertained that there was plenty of whisky.)

Esau rose to oppose the remarks of the honourable gentleman. 'Such self-denial would be a good action, but the constant performance of virtuous actions tends to make one haughty. I dare say you fellows don't know this, but I do, because I've tried it. I prefer to be wicked and humble.'

The motion was not pressed to a division.

We are well provided with all kinds of food, for we found in the larder a shoulder of venison, and we have any amount of ryper, which, as John says, 'will save our bacon, though they could not save their own;' and so with a comfortable hut to live in, a river full of fish at our door, and a blazing fire to sit round, life assumes a rosy hue, and we go to sleep in real beds with bright hopes of the future.

The Skipper was heard to murmur as he turned over to sleep, ' I say, what bread that is! When I get home I shall publish a pamphlet, and teach all the world to bake like that.'

It is rather rough on the Skipper's pamphlet to publish his recipe here, but this is copied from his journal:—

'Take dough in large quantities and place it on a tin. Heat the oven till you are sick to death of piling on wood. Smoke a pipe, and remove the ashes. Place the dough in the oven, and leave home for an indefinite period. If you ever return, remove the decomposed particles, and let them get warm in the sun, or else freeze in the snow, it really don't matter a bit. Now heat the oven and recommit them. Brood over the oven, exhibiting the tenderest solicitude. They will soon be done, and perhaps will be good, perhaps not; nobody can tell.'

September 9.—Last night was very cold, and this morning there was ice on the lake, and the bilge-water in the boat was frozen solid. Esau and Jens went up the lake in the boat to stalk, and the Skipper accompanied them to fish, while John fished nearer home.

About six o'clock the boat was seen returning loaded with the head and skin of a very fine buck, and Esau gave us his history thus:—

'As soon as we landed halfway up the lake we found the spoor of two very large bucks and a smaller one which had swum across the lake in the night. They seemed to have gone towards the Tyknings glacier, so we went in that direction also. The wind was as bad as it could be in that valley, for we were obliged to walk exactly with it at first instead of against it, in order to get round a sufficiently large piece of country, and then work back against the wind. We walked a couple of miles without seeing anything, and at last got close to the Tyknings glacier and the iceberg lake at its foot. You know that lake well enough, Skipper, full of lumps of ice, some of them as big as this hut, which keep breaking off from the projecting glacier as it slides down, and I dare say you remember what an awful deathly stillness reigns there and what a dismal sight the lake is, cold and black under the shade of the crags which close in its sides.

'Well, we sat down there and used the glasses for a long time'——

'What do you mean by "using the glasses"?' interrupted John; 'drinking whisky and water?'

Esau withered him with a look and went on.

'Well, "spied," if you like, spied for a long time without seeing anything; and we had just walked on again a few yards, when the silence was suddenly broken by a cry from Jens of "Reins," and there, 300 yards in front of us, was a noble buck which had evidently been concealed from our view by some rocks, and had now smelt us and was departing at a stately trot; apparently despising undignified hurry.

'I fancy his intention was to trot away at that long swinging pace, and get into Asiatic Russia in time for tea; so I grabbed the rifle from Jens, as of course, now that he was alarmed, a long shot was our only chance; sat down on a stone, and with the faintest hopes of hitting him, fired twice, and, of course, missed.

'Now here was where my luck came in. If that buck had not been so proud, he could have run straight away from us to the glacier beyond the lake, but we were "betwixt the wind and his nobility," and he wanted to get a clean breeze, and run against it instead of down it. Consequently, when he was about 350 yards away he turned to the right, apparently intending to make a circle round us, and so get the wind in his face.

'Directly he turned broadside to us Jens gave a shrill whistle, and the buck stopped short for a moment, so that I had just time to make a careful shot, and the bullet hit him in the ribs. At the shot he stumbled, but recovered himself instantly, and made off a good deal faster than before, evidently perceiving that things were getting serious, and that "this here warn't no child's play." Before I could fire again he got into the ravine which runs down towards Rus Lake, and was out of our sight.

'We thought there was just a chance of cutting him off in that extremely rough ground, though, of course, we could not tell whether he was much hurt or not; so we ran as hard as we could for about a quarter of a mile, loading as we ran. Suddenly I caught sight of him going very slowly, but luckily he did not see us, so we dodged into a little gully, and after another short run came in sight of him standing still, no doubt owing to his wound, and about 250 yards away.

'This time he saw us, and darted off as fleetly as ever, no longer with his side to us, but straight away. I was dead beat, and Jens had thrown himself down, and was panting like—like'——

'A concertina?' suggested the Skipper.

'Yes, just so. Anyhow, we could not run another yard; you know what it is on those stones, so I sat down again, and with the rifle going like a pump-handle, fired, and, by the greatest luck, hit him close to the tail, and the bullet went clean through his body and smashed his shoulder. Down he went, and we raised a yell of triumph, whereupon he jumped up again and went off at a slapping pace in a most extraordin-

ary manner. I believe if he could have reached the snow he would have done us even now but we were between him and the glacier, and he had nothing but rocks to go on, bad enough for a deer with the proper complement of legs and ribs, and very trying indeed to one crippled like this, I'm sure.

'However, he kept going at a great pace for a few hundred yards, and we lay in a state of exhaustion and watched him through the glass. Soon he began to move more slowly, and then to go round and round in a small circle, and at last he lay down. By that time I had partially recovered my wind, so I stalked him with great care and got within a hundred yards of him, took a steady aim for his heart, and pulled. To my horror he bounced up again, and ran like a hare for a dozen yards, and then rolled over and over as dead as Julius Cæsar.

'How Jens and I whooped and shook hands and laughed can be imagined by any one who has seen a grand deer almost escape him, and then, by a bit of luck and a breakneck run, just nailed him when the chance seemed hopeless. After that we lay on our backs and panted for some time, but after finishing the whisky and a large portion of the iceberg lake we recovered sufficiently to skin our prize and cut him up. He is a most splendidly fat "stor bock," Jens says by far the best that has been killed in these parts this year; a beautiful skin, and, best luck of all, his horns have got rid of the velvet, and are fit to take home: and they have fourteen points. I measured the fat on his loins, and it was two and a half inches thick. Jens tried to bring home a hind quarter as well as the head and skin, but before he had gone twenty yards he found that it was too much for him, so turned back and buried it with the rest.'

We have obtained some interesting information from Jens about the horns of the reindeer. As every one knows, both the bucks and does have horns, but they shed them at different times: those of the does and smaller bucks are now in velvet, and will not get properly hard until October; they will then remain on all through the winter, and be shed in the spring. But the large bucks have their horns hard now, and will shed them in the winter, and so be defenceless during the time when the snow lies thickest.

All this is undoubtedly true, for Jens is thoroughly trustworthy in his facts, but what is the reason?

Jens does not know, but he gives us another fact. In the winter, when the 'stor bocks' have no horns, the snow is often so deep that only the strongest deer can scrape it away to lay bare the moss which at that season forms their food. Then come the does and smaller bucks, and with their horns push away the unfortunate big ones, and so are saved from starvation, while the ill-treated 'stor bocks' have to work double tides in order to get anything to eat.

We present this fact in all humility to Mr. Darwin as a solution of the problem, 'Why has the female reindeer horns?' Evidently, they originally had none, but by constant pushing at their lords and masters they developed them by degrees; then, by the survival of the fittest, those does with the longest and sharpest horns prospered most, and soon there were none of the hornless does left, and all calves began to have horns as a matter of course.

CHAPTER XXX.

NOT LOST, BUT GONE BEFORE.

September 12.—Early this morning we sorrowfully packed the Skipper's things on the pony, and then we three and Ola marched off down the river towards civilisation. The Skipper hoped to get over about twenty-five miles before night; Esau wanted to try the river a long way down; and John said he 'always liked a stroll on Sunday,' and with that object accompanied the Skipper for the first eleven miles of his journey, returning to Rusvasoset in time for dinner.

About four miles below Rus Lake, the river, which is there about thirty yards wide, suddenly disappears into a narrow cleft in the rocky bed, and runs in this curious rift for several hundred yards, and then again emerges into daylight. The sides of this rocky prison are just over a yard apart at the narrowest place, though the gap only appears to be a few inches wide; but the force with which the immense body of water is squeezed through the tortuous passage far down below, whirling huge boulders along with irresistible force, and covering the surrounding rocks with moisture from the ever-rising misty spray, makes it a severe trial to the nerves to step across the cleft; the ceaseless din of the rushing water is of itself sufficiently appalling.

This channel has evidently been gradually worn down through the solid rock, which here appears to be a reef of softer nature than the usual formation of this country. On the top and in niches all the way down are still to be seen the turn holes caused by stones working round and round in an eddy; but the curious fact is that while at the top the cleft is only a yard across, it widens regularly out as it gets deeper, and at the bottom is fully ten yards in width. Now it seems unlikely that the Russen river could ever have been content to run in a bed so much narrower than its present one, and from the appearance of the strata we imagine that as it worked down and undermined the cliffs at each side, they have gradually toppled forward to meet each other. Probably soon they will actually touch, after which a very short time will see the natural arch so formed covered with vegetation, and the river will run in a subterranean passage.

Through this channel no fish could pass alive, so there Esau bade 'farvel' to the Skipper, and, encumbered with rod and fishing bag, leaped like a goat across the intervening Devil's Dyke, and was soon lost to view as he fished his way up stream.

The other two pursued their journey steadily, and found it pleasant to gradually walk down from the Scotch mist which overhung everything up at Rus Vand, into, firstly, dull dry weather just below the clouds, and then a little further into real sunshine and warmth. About one o'clock they reached Hind Sæter, the tenants of which were still there, but just in the act of removing to the valley. Here they feasted together on fladbrod, and then the things were packed on a cart, and the Skipper, following them as they jolted away under Ola's guidance through the pine forest, was seen no more by his disconsolate comrade.

When John returned to Rusvasoset a little before dinner-time, we found it necessary to bake bread and a pie, our invariable rule 'when in doubt.' This was not a case that admitted of any hesitation, for the Skipper had taken all the food that he could annex for his sustenance on the journey, as he did not expect to find any people in the sæters on his path.

The evening was spent in general tidying, and mending various articles which had gone wrong; holes in landing-nets, rents in trousers and coats, and inserting new screws in Esau's boots for the stalk he hoped, but hardly expected, to make on the morrow. At night the outlook was anything but encouraging, dense clouds folding all nature in their cold embrace, and the pitiless rain beating down on our poor little hut as if it took a pleasure in the occupation.

September 13.—Rain, and nothing but rain.

September 14.—We never knew when sunrise and daybreak took place to-day, or whether they happened at all, for the prospect was more hopeless than ever, and the rain still fell with unabated vigour.

We were at the end of our indoor resources, but fortunately Ola returned with some English papers which he had found waiting for us at Ransværk, the sæter at which he and the Skipper passed the night, and at which this bundle of literature had been deposited about a fortnight ago by the latest traveller from Vaage. But for this, there would certainly have been bloodshed in this remote spot, our tempers not being equal to the strain of two days in succession without being able to see ten yards in front of us, or to stir out without becoming waterlogged.

Even the fish were apparently at last disgusted at not being able to get into a dry corner by jumping out of the water, and our efforts to persuade them to try the interior of a waterproof bag only met with indifferent success.

The stubborn resistance of our well-tried roof has at last been overcome, and soon after turning in last night we had to turn out again to rig up various hydrostatic appliance- with a view to diverting the course of some of the supers fluous rainfall, and irrigating the floor therewith instead of

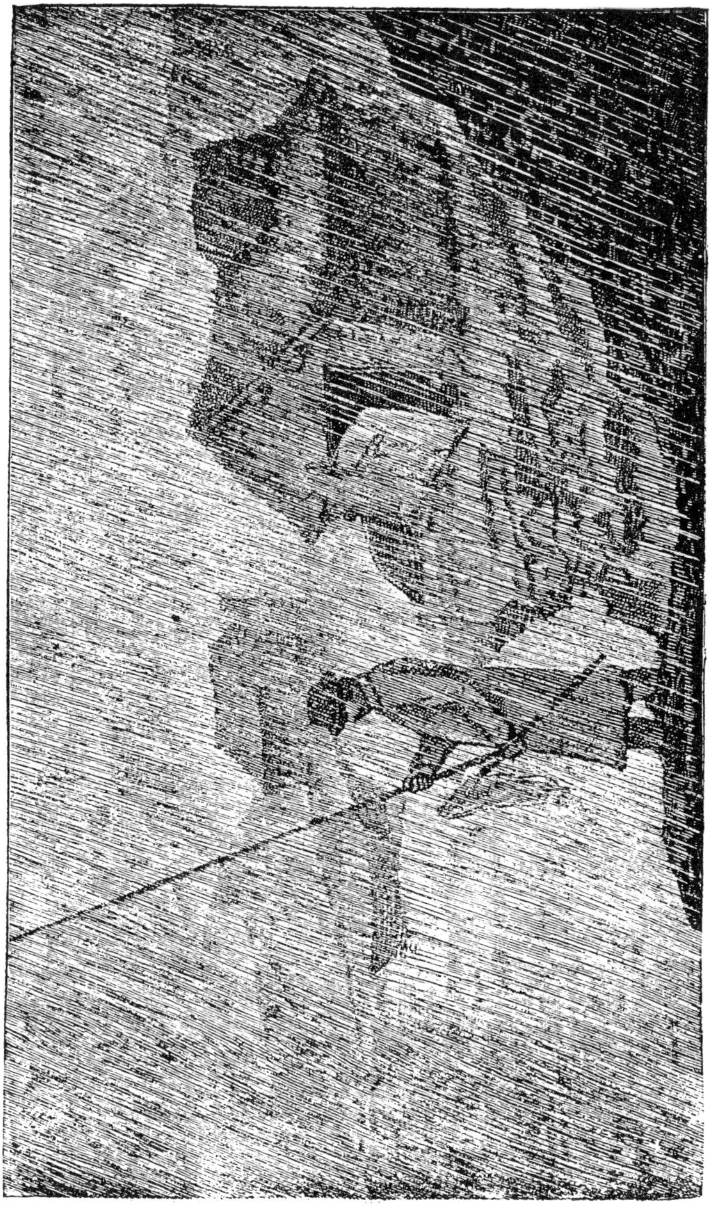

letting the beds get it all. The latter really needed it much less than the boards, which were somewhat dusty; but probably the mistake arose from John sitting on one of them while he mixed the dough, so that it might have been taken for a flour-bed.

September 15.—At last we were relieved by a change in the wind, soon followed by a cessation of rain, and then the mist began to lift, and by noon the sun was actually beginning to glimmer feebly, and the mountains to be visible for half their height.

John went on a general tour of mountaineering and prospecting in search of scenery, and came back delighted with himself, having made a higher climb than usual, and seen Nautgardstind in all the perfect beauty with which the newly fallen snow had endowed him.

It has already been mentioned that John does *not* like walking uphill, and when he makes a self-sacrificing and voluntary ascent as he did to-day, he comes home brimming over with an excess of conscious virtue which does not pass away until the genial influence of a good meal and a pipe has reduced him to the level of all humanity.

On his way home he heard a feeble squeak in a bush, and peering in discovered a small animal which he at first took for a guinea-pig; but soon, perceiving that it must be a lemming, his natural impulse was to poke it with a stick. This was his first interview with one, though they are common enough up here; and he is disposed to think them morose in disposition; but really he ought to have recognised the fact that the thin end of a walking-stick is not a means of intercourse at all likely to arouse the sympathy of any animal, least of all that of a juvenile lemming, who is obviously overcome with drowsiness, and wants to be let alone.

The winter is now coming on apace, and already every fall of rain down here is a snowstorm in the mountains, and every clear night means a biting frost up there. Esau, scaling the heights of Bes Hø with Jens in search of deer, found none on account of the mist, and in addition to the danger of getting lost, a new peril was added by the snow. It appeared that during the night a severe frost had immediately followed the rain and coated everything with ice, then snow had fallen to the depth of three inches, and on the top of that rain and sharp frost again. The result was that at every step they broke through the crust of ice on the top, and sank through the three inches of soft snow on to the lower stratum of ice. This was all very well as long as they were on rough ground; but the snow making every place look the same, in one instance

they got on to one of the steep little glaciers which are common on Bes Hø, without knowing that they had done so: and suddenly Jens lost his footing and began to slide downwards at a terrific speed. It seemed to Esau that he would shoot straight down into Rus Vand, looking very blue and cold three thousand feet below; but a friendly boulder intervened, and by its assistance, and by spreading himself out like a gigantic spider, he managed to arrest his wild career, and they got safe across the treacherous glacier.

They had to cross another on their return, which was done with fear and trembling; but although the difficulties of this kind of stalking when unaccompanied by deer may seem to outnumber the pleasures, still occasionally they were on

fairly safe ground, and could get their hearts out of their mouths for a few brief moments. At such times the spendid view of all our old Gjendin mountains rising tier after tier behind each other, a boundless sea of peaks and domes and jagged crags, all robed in purest white, with the sun lighting up the virgin snow almost too brightly for the eye to rest on; the keen frosty air; and the solemn stillness, only broken now and again by the twittering of a flock of snow buntings, amply repaid them for the arduous climb.

Then a few minutes of glorious excitement as, by the aid of glissades, they shot down the steeps that it had needed hours of hard labour to surmount, and they were back on the shores of Rus Vand, where at present the snow had hardly begun to lie.

In spite of the cold we had some first-rate fishing, and Esau caught a trout which he asserted to be the very best fish for shape, condition, and colour, that ever came out of Rus Lake, or anywhere else. Though not as large as many we have caught, being only 2½ lbs., it certainly was a beauty, and resembled the perfect fish that are occasionally seen in an oil painting, but very seldom encountered in tangible, edible form.

The Rus trout, like those of Gjendin, are quite silvery, almost as bright as a salmon, but with a few pink spots instead of black ones, and uncommonly pretty they look when fresh out of the water.

Too soon evening put an end to our sport, and when the last rays of the setting sun had tinted the distant snow with a delicate pink hue which lingered, paled, and faded as the cold silvery light of the moon began to assert its sway, the keen air drove us home, and made us content to enjoy from the hut door the lovely clear night which succeeded so bright a day.

CHAPTER XXXI.

HOMEWARD BOUND.

September 17.—Our ears were gladdened by the sound of Ivar's hoarse cachinnation some time during the night or early morning, and on turning out he informed us that he should have been here yesterday, but his cart had been smashed on the road beyond Hind Sæter; however, he had patched it up and got it to the sæter; so we distributed our goods on the two ponies, after seizing our last chance of a 'square meal,' by eating an enormous breakfast of venison pie, cutlets, and trout.

All our stores came to an end yesterday, except candles and soap. The latter article has for some time been lying in great bars on a shelf as a reproach to us, and we were glad to get it out of our sight to-day, and 'give it to the men,' as we would anything else that is repulsive to our feelings. There were a few scraps of other delicacies which we divided among the retainers, and then taking with us a fore-quarter of 'stor bock' for our own consumption on the journey, and a hind-quarter carefully sewn up in the sail of Esau's canoe, and intended as a present for Mr. Thomas, we regretfully took leave of the little hut, and started for Besse Sæter.

Ola and Jens were sent down the Russen River, which is the nearest way to Hind Sæter; and Ivar was to meet us at the eastern end of Sjødals Lake as soon as he could get there.

We paused at the brow of the hill to have a last look at the beautiful lake and quaint little huts, and to take off our hats to grand old Nautgardstind, to whom we hoped we were not bidding an eternal 'farvel;' and then we turned across the fjeld, and, losing sight of the Rus valley, were soon looking forward again to the change and uncertainty of the home-ward journey.

From Besse Sæter, which was reached at noon, we launched our craft into the lake with a nasty sidewind blowing, which delayed our progress considerably, so that we took an hour to reach the lower end of the lake, a distance of not quite four miles.

There we found Ivar with his pony and sleigh, on which the canoe was conveyed to the junction of the Sjoa and Russen Rivers, where Esau launched her again and ran the rapids down to Ruslien Sæter, a very fine bit of stream, in which the canoe could only just manage to live.

Finding that the sæter girls were still here, we went in and asked for milk. They suggested cream: amendment carried without a division. A huge bowl of the thickest and most delicious cream was set before us, which we, armed with two enormous spoons, attacked and soon consumed utterly, with an indefinite amount of fladbrod and cheese. Charge for the whole, sixpence! We have no hesitation in saying that the cream alone would have been worth its weight in gold in Piccadilly.

We then regained our craft, and had a delightful cruise down to Hind Sæter, the stream going at millrace speed all the way, so that we did the two and a half miles in fifteen minutes, arriving long before our cavalcade of men and ponies, who started twenty minutes before us, while we were discussing the cream.

The sæter was deserted for the winter, but Ivar produced his cart from the bed of a stream where he had left it to improve the wheels, and at half-past five we, with Jens and one cart, resumed our journey, leaving the other two men with the canoe to follow us.

We had originally intended to make the journey to Lillehammer from here entirely by canoe down the Sjoa until it joined the Laagen, but the premature departure of the Skipper knocked that little scheme on the head.

It would have been a tremendous enterprise, for the Sjoa is such a turbulent river that there would have been a great deal of portage to be done; but we had agreed to allow a fortnight for it, and were looking forward to it with great delight. The Laagen is a fairly navigable river all the way, with the exception of a few very large falls; but there is a good road by its side, so that we should have had no difficulty if we had been lucky enough ever to reach it. However,

> 'The best laid schemes o' mice an' men
> Gang aft a-gley;'

and we were reduced to the prosaic necessity of walking, and helping to hold our luggage on to a jolting cart.

As we gradually descended into the birch-woods we were much struck by the beautiful effects of the variegated autumn tints, and soon the brilliant reds and yellows of the birches began to contrast with the dark green of the fir trees, the light greyish green of the lichen, and rich brown and purple of the ground and undergrowth. It was so long since we had seen any trees, that their beauty seemed to come to us quite as a new sensation.

Below Hind Sæter the road lay through dense forests of pines for mile after mile, with hardly any change except where we got occasional glimpses of the Sjoa tearing madly along far beneath us—so far that only a faint murmur came up from the leaping, hurrying waters. Hour after hour we walked, and still the same dark forest gloomed above us, so remote from the busy haunts of men that it seems not to be worth any one's while to cut the trees except for use in the immediate neighbourhood, and hundreds of them lie naked and dead as they have fallen before the fury of the gale, and slowly rot or are devoured by insects until their place is ready for a successor.

As the shades of evening began to close, we were several times startled as the huge body of a capercailzie darted across the road at a pace which seemed impossible to such an enormous bird, and with an absence of noise that appeared equally unnatural.

About half-past eight we came to a more open part of the forest, and soon we saw a glimmering light ahead: Jens cheerily said, 'Randsværk;' and in a few more minutes we pulled up at the door of a large sæter.

Without knocking Jens opened the door, and we walked in

and struck a light. There was the usual fireplace and table, and in the further corner a bed, which, as we presently perceived, was occupied by two girls. This discovery embarrassed us a little; but no one else, least of all the girls themselves, appeared to be at all disconcerted.

In our favoured land a woman would probably be slightly concerned if she were aroused from sleep by the unceremonious entrance into her room of three men, two of them ruffianly-looking strangers of foreign exterior; but not so these artless beings. The elder one at once got out of bed and proceeded to dress, while her sister remained where she was and soon fell asleep.

When the dressing commenced, we, being innocent young bachelors, retired and remained outside till it was finished but we do not believe she appreciated our delicacy at all.

Then this poor girl, no doubt very tired after a hard day's work at cheese-making, proceeded to relight the fire, prepare coffee, and broil some venison for us. And just as we finished a hearty meal, Ola and Ivar arrived, so that she had to begin all over again for them. Finally, in spite of our remonstrances, she dragged her sister out of the bed, and insisted on our having it, while they went and slept in another building a few yards away. So John took the bed they had vacated, while Esau made a couch for himself in the cheese-room, and we slept the sleep of the hardworked, virtuous, penniless wanderer.

Verily they have a better idea in Norway of true hospitality than in any other country under the sun.

September 18.—How strange that our return to the haunts of men should be chiefly marked by the sparseness of the fare provided for breakfast! A tin of sardines took the place of the usual trout; and although Ransværk consists of a group of several sæters, and almost attains to the dignity of a village, and our quarters were in the largest and most imposing mansion, there were no forks or spoons to be obtained, and we had to fish our sardines out of their native oil with a Tollekniv, assisted by a finger, and convey them to our mouths with the same implements.

Our route to-day through the forest was most beautiful, at one time descending to the level of the Sjoa, and even struggling along its bed where the going on the bank seemed to be inferior, at another climbing up and up and ever higher, until we stood on the summit of the range of hills which confine this valley on the northern side. It is called Hedalen, and is one of those strikingly beautiful half-cultivated Norwegian dales which occupy the space between civilisation and the untouched realms of nature.

This evening, the setting sun throwing a rich golden glow over the scene, and lighting up the brilliant autumnal colours of the trees, gave us an opportunity of seeing it quite at its best.

Gradually the forest began to get more open, and the road to improve. Several peasants in picturesque garb were seen on the wayside: rough buildings became more frequent, and fields and fences quite common; at first only pasture land, but soon cornfields and patches of potatoes.

Then at last in the twilight we make a swift descent from the ridge along which the road runs; a short plunge through a thicket, down a grassy track; a bridge over a little stream; and as we breast the opposite bank, a pile of buildings looming in front and looking perfectly gigantic to our eyes, so long accustomed to the tiniest of huts; and Jens points up, cracks his whip, and says, 'Bjølstad.' The pony boils up something like 'a trot for the avenue,' and rattles the cart into a large square courtyard, tenanted only by two huge dogs; and as a cheery old Norseman rushes out in great excitement to welcome us and lead us into a bright, clean, curtained room, we feel that we have said farewell to the delights of savage life, and will probably have to put on a necktie to-morrow.

Here we parted with our faithful Jens, and very sorry we were to do so, as we think him a first-rate fellow: a man with a bright eye and stolid demeanour; naturally silent, but game for anything; a keen sportsman and wonderful stalker, and without a particle of the laziness and sulkiness which characterised Ola.

Here, for the first time since leaving Lillehammer in July, we slept between sheets.

Our own and only Ivar has volunteered to what he calls 'transportare' all our baggage in his cart down to Lillehammer, distant about eighty miles hence, for the sum of twenty-two shillings. This sounds unreasonable, but it was his own suggestion, so we did not argue the point, only stipulating that he should be there by noon on Tuesday, to-day being Saturday, and leaving the details to him.

Our thoughts were here recalled to the Skipper and his adventures by finding the following note from him:—

'DEAR ESAU,—I have left behind me here certain of what the Romans so appropriately called "impedimenta" and hope that you will be able to bring them home for me. I got an old, old man with a small cart to bring my luggage down from Ransværk. It was a wet day. I walked the first nine miles while the old man and the rain were both driving. This ancient driveller seemed to imagine it was a fine day, and had hung on his best coat and hat, further aggravating his appearance with a spotted kerchief and a light heart. He seemed remarkably cheerful, as carolling he drove his carjole and cajoled his horse through the dripping pine forests. I arrived here at midday, and the owner, Ivar Tofte, came out to meet me. He took a great fancy to me, and we finished together a bottle of the most delicious aquavit, which he produced from a cellar where it had been laid down in the time of the Vikings. It is a pity neither of you can speak the language!—Yours haughtily,

'THE SKIPPER.'

We found that the 'impedimenta' of which the Skipper had spoken were 147 loaded cartridges wrapped up in a flannel shirt, the whole being enveloped in a partially cured reindeer-skin.

We were further reminded of our lost one by looking in the Day-book (or traveller's name-book), where his was the last English name. This was not surprising, for though Bjølstad is a posting station, it is a very out-of-the-way place; but we looked back for two years without finding that any other Englishman had been here, and then the Skipper's name occurred again. Between these dates the names were all Norwegian, and there were not very many even of them.

CHAPTER XXXII.

BJØLSTAD.

Sunday, September 19.—Bjølstad is an ancient Norwegian homestead, and consists of several separate buildings surrounding a central rectangular court. The house that we slept in bears the date of 1818, and is the most modern as well as the largest of the group; it is really a suite of state apartments for the use of the King on the rare occasions when he visits this part of his dominions.

On the left-hand side of the courtyard, as we stand at the door of our state apartments, is a very quaint and picturesque old house with a handsome porch, built in the Byzantine style, date 1743, and in this the owner lives whenever he comes to this farm.

Opposite to us is another building even more curious in its architecture, and considerably older than the other; and the remaining side of the yard is occupied by another more modern edifice used chiefly as a storehouse. Besides these there are several other detached outbuildings, in which sleighs, ploughs, spare cooking utensils, rugs, and various other useful and useeless articles are kept, including all the fittings and even the weathercock of an ancient church which used to stand close to the farm, but which is now demolished and partly reduced to firewood.

The owner of all this grandeur is one Ivar Tofte, a wealthy yeoman who has several other farms in other parts of the country, one of which is much larger and more important even than Bjølstad; and we were lucky enough to find this Northern Crœsus at home, for it turned out that he was the cheery old man in the shocking bad hat who had run out to welcome us last night.

This morning he came into our room after breakfast, with a bottle of aquavit in his hand wherewith to drink our health. Now to refuse this ceremony is an unpardonable insult, but we had tasted aquavit before, and had a wholesome dread of the nauseous compound, reeking of carraway seeds and aniseed, which we were accustomed to expect out of an aquavit bottle. So we poured out very small glasses, clinked them in approved manner, and raised them to our lips as we uttered the magic word Skaal, more with a feeling of disgust than any other sensation. And then it was beautiful to see a heavenly smile steal over Esau's ingenuous countenance; while John, softly murmuring, 'Chartreuse, by George!' reached for the

bottle, and with a shout of 'Skaal Ivar Tofte,' proceeded to fill himself a bumper. It was a perfect liqueur, soft, delicate, and mellow, as probably age alone could have made it; and we drank Skaal to 'Gammle Norge,' and England, and Kong Oscar, and Queen Vict*oo*ria, and Ivar Tofte again, and then ourselves again; whereupon the old man perceived that we appreciated his 'cuvée de réserve,' and went for another full bottle, which he left in our room, so that we could 'put it to our lips when we felt so disposed.'

After this, John, feeling at once genial and liberal, announced his intention of buying a sheenfelt (sheepskin rug) for importation into England; and Tofte with an aged retainer volunteered to show us his stores of sheepskins.

First our guide procured a bunch of enormous keys, such as Bluebeard would have hanging from his waist in a pantomime, labelled 'Key of the Wine-cellar. Umbrella stand. Fowl-house. Potted shrimps. Cupboard where the jam's kept,' &c., &c. Then he marched off to one of the buildings, followed by us and the other old man, whose profession was apparently to exalt Bjølstad sheenfelts, and to debase—as far as extreme volubility and strict inattention to the elements of truth would enable him to accomplish that object—an ancient one which John wished to give in part payment.

Bluebeard led us up some stairs to the Blue Chamber, where we saw hanging in a row the skins, not of his deceased wives, but of many 'timid-glancing, herbage-cropping, fleecy flocks,' to use the beautiful and touching language of the Greek poet. Then the two accomplices selected the sheenfelt which they intended us to buy, and began to expatiate on its beauties in terms of undisguised admiration; and after half an hour's huckstering and haggling, of course they persuaded John to take that and no other. However, it was a beautiful specimen of this kind of rug, of a dark grey colour, and very thick, warm, and heavy; so both sides were highly satisfied, and proceeded to the drinking of more aquavit in celebration of the bargain.

The weather was so unpleasant, and Bluebeard and his aquavit were so engaging, that we decided not to leave here till to-morrow. Our host was delighted to hear this, and at once went for more aquavit, which he appears to consider the first necessity of life; and then he proceeded to show us round his ancestral halls, at though he were a sober old verger of Westminster Abbey.

There was a sort of old-world Rip van Winkle sleepiness about Bjølstad very soothing to men who like us have lived in the nineteenth century for some few years. All the varlets and handmaidens were dressed in the old native costume, so appropriate to the ancient wooden buildings with quaintly carved eaves and doorways, about which they hovered. In the courtyard were two enormous dogs, that barked loudly whenever we appeared, but at the same time wagged their tails and looked imbecile and good-natured. There were also four geese, who meant to be sitting basking in the rain, but as soon as anybody came to one of the numerous doors, or crossed the yard, they all stood up and quacked solemnly fourteen times each, then hissed once, and sat down again; and as some one was always moving about the court, the quiet rest of those birds was more anticipatory than real; but they alone of all the living creatures at Bjølstad appeared to have any fixed employment which demanded constant attention.

Bluebeard first took us through the state apartments, which contained many curious and interesting things of all ages, from an axe nearly a thousand years old, to a Birmingham plated teapot won at the Christiania horse show in 1860.

The Toftes boast themselves descended from Harald Haarfager, and are so proud of their ancestry, that from time immemorial they have never married out of their own family. If dear old Bluebeard may be accepted as an ordinary result of this system, it must be confessed that it has its advantages.

The things that he chiefly delighted to show us were those which had been used by the King during his occasional visits, the most curious being a large stone table made of one enormous slab not more than three-quarters of an inch thick, but very hard and elastic, more like a steel plate than stone; gorgeously embroidered counterpanes and chairs; some very old ploughs and sleighs; and a brass-bound box with a marvellous representation of Adam and Eve, very evidently before the Fall, and the most remarkable thing in serpents which the wildest flight of human imagination has yet conceived. There were some very nice silver utensils and ornaments, but not many, as most of his plate is kept at his largest farm. All that he had here was in a cupboard with a rubbishy unlocked deal door, standing in John's bedroom; a fact which speaks volumes for the trusting simplicity and total inability to read a man's character from his appearance, caused by a millennium of marrying your cousin once removed. Poor Bluebeard! he little thought what a viper he was nurturing in his bosom, or rather in his chest (his plate-chest), and that in that room lay one who could perhaps, if he would, answer the questions—

Who took the Gainsborough?
Who has the Dudley diamonds?
Who stole the donkey? and
Where's the cat?

N.B.—John has now a large collection of ancient Norwegian silver, counterpanes, belts, tankards knives, and ornaments to dispose of at very low prices if no questions are asked. —ADVT.

September 20.—We left Bjølstad in carioles on a real road about nine o'clock, Bluebeard himself assisting in the operation of harnessing the ponies and packing the baggage. Just as we were driving off, a brilliantly original idea occured to him, and he said, 'Come in and taste my aquavit.' We did not like to refuse an old grey-haired man's simple request, so descended and drank another Skaal to all the usual loyal, patriotic, and festive toasts, and then we drove off murmuring somewhat indistinctly, 'Shkaal Iva' Tofte Shhkaal Iv Toffic Shko Toffy. Jolly good fler-oleshole-Toffy.'

All day we drove, and ever as we descended the Hedalen valley with the noisy Sjoa on our right hand, the farming kept improving, and the country becoming more populous; and we saw many families digging potaoes, many pigs roaming free and unmolested as they do in Ireland, and a few men bringing up store from the town for the long season of snowed-up dreariness now so near at hand. Jens told us that in winter, even so far to the south as Vaage, the sun only rises about eleven, and sets at one o'clock, giving barely three hours of daylight in midwinter; though he said that in the mountains where he spends his time hunting, there is rather more light than in the valleys.

For three hours we followed the brawling Sjoa through scenery that would bear comparison with Switerzerland, and then we reached the spot where it joins the mighty Laagen, and crossing the latter by a picturesque but discouraging bridge, soon struck the main road, and pulled up for our first change of ponies at Storklevstad, nineteen miles from Bjølstad.

At another place further on we found a shop kept by a Norwegian Yankee, and entered it to buy some sugar-candy, wherewith to appease our cariole-boy. This storekeeper informed us that the emigration from Norway to the States was enormous just now, especially to Minnesota and Wisconsin, and that no less then sixteen men had gone this year from the little village of Vaage—a place which does not strike one as being likely to contain that number of able-bodied men at one time. Ola had told us that five of his brethren were in Minnesota, but that he himself had no intention of leaving his native country; and this we thought to be well, for if he were to join them we are convinced that any enterprise in which they might be engaged would inevitably fail with his invaluable co-operation and assistance—unless perhaps the Skipper could be induced to go out there and occasionally exhort him.

At Listad we lunched off a real white tablecloth; that is to say, we ate not the cloth, but everything eatable that was placed on it.

We also found a note from the Skipper asking us to bring along one or two little things that he had been obliged to leave behind in his hurried flight, just as the allied armies kept finding Napoleon's belongings at different places after Waterloo. The present loot consisted of a coat, sleeping rug, and a towel.

At Kirkestuen we quitted the track for the night, having made fifty miles in about ten hours. This, according to our experience, is a fair rate of progression in Norway; in fact, the traveller is more likely to find the average below this than above, unless he drives the good little ponies faster than they like to go, which is wrong.

Here the three women who kept the station were immensely amused because we asked for coffee with our food, and one of them took upon herself the task of rebuking us for such dissipated habits, and explained at great length that no respectable people ever did such a thing. 'Coffee,' she said, 'should only be drunk during the day, gruel after sunset.' But we persisted in our reckless demand, and they finally gave in, and produced the delicious compound that may be expected at any wretched little dwelling throughout the country.

CHAPTER XXXIII.

DOWN TO CHRISTIANIA.

September 21.—The steadily improving weather of our homeward journey is very pleasant, and already we are beginning to almost forget those 'Miseries in Cold and Grey' which were so conspicuous during our last few days at Rus Vand.

To-day we noticed that the whole population of the country appeared to be engaged in the seductive pastime of potato-digging. One family that we passed consisted of papa, mamma, and eight children of different ages, all absorbed in this pursuit. The parents had gardening tools, the elder children were using pickaxes and trowels, the younger ones fireshovels and wooden baking spades, and the mere babies were hard at work with spoons and toasting-forks.

Here and there we detected a few people still making hay, presumably because they had no potatoes. In Norway the hill-sides are so steep and rocky that there is not overmuch room for the cultivation of grass, so they have to collect it from every available corner where a few sprays of anything green can contrive to exist. As we have mentioned, they are now curing grass on the house-tops, and to-day we saw a man with a scythe about eighteen inches long, mowing in amongst the stones on the river bank, and in some of the places where he went the scythe blade was the only blade visible to the naked eye. One thing seems certain, that a Norwegian *will* make hay while the sun shines, even if he can only find rocks out of which to make it.

Ever as we followed the almost imperceptible descent of the road, the great river Laagen became wider, deeper, and bluer, as it gathered increased volume from the numberless tributaries which flow into it from every hill, till at length at Fossegaarden it plunged over a series of ledges in a splendid succession of falls, and after winding awhile amid fir-clad islands and shaded grassy banks, it flowed into the Mjøsen Lake and was lost, while we on the road above, rounding the last corner and turning to the east, soon found ourselves in Lillehammer, which really looked quite a towny little town.

Esau stopped at Fossegaarden a couple of hours to throw a fly in the tempting-looking water below the falls, and was rewarded at the first cast by a rise from a fish whose peculiar wriggling and rolling soon showed him to be a grayling; and before leaving, the bag was filled with some very fine specimens of this beautiful and delicate fish.

We were greeted as old friends at the Victoria Hotel, where Ivar had already arrived with our things. Then we ordered our own dinner, and told the host to supply Ivar with whatever he wanted regardless of expense (the result of this reckless munificence was a bill for nearly two shillings); and in the happy frame of mind produced on both sides by this course we settled our accounts with him, and giving him all our worn-out garments and some candles and matches, we parted with the last of our henchmen.

By the way, we here found a note from the Skipper asking us to bring home a pair of shooting boots, three socks, and the remains of what had apparently been a pocket handkerchief; but the obvious course that suggested itself was 'give 'em to the men,' and we insisted on Ivar taking these valuables.

September 22.—With the utmost difficulty, by threats and coercion Esau was induced to leave his bed, and dragged to the steamer in time for her derparture, as, if left to his own inclinations, he would have remained in his insidious couch until this globe had performed its diurnal revolution.

As it was, the 'Skibladner' was indulging in a final premonitory shriek before leaving the pier when we came hurrying and stumbling down the hill at all paces, and we only stepped aboard just as she threw off the last detaining rope.

The steamer was at first very empty, but more people joined us at every stopping-place, of which there are about a dozen on the lake. Some of these are little villages, with only the bright roofs and church spire peeping out from among the fir trees; others no more than a landing-stage projecting into the blue waters, and no other indications of life save perhaps a couple of idle fishing boats and a flagstaff.

The morning was so calm and fine, that the grayling playing under the shore made the only break in the otherwise unruffled surface of the lake, and it seemed strange to find ourselves back in summer again, having left winter with its snow and frosts far above us up at Rus Vand only a few days ago.

At Hamar some English people came aboard, so that we had some one to talk to. At every place where the steamer stopped and fresh passengers came off in boats to meet us, it seemed to be customary that they should take off their hats to the captain on the bridge as they pulled up alongside: even when we passed the smallest places without stopping, merely throwing the mail bag into a boat as we darted by, the fresh-water sailors on the steamer all took off their hats to the fresh-water sailors ashore, the latter always returning the salutation; and considering the fact that two steamers pass every day, this indicates no small degree of politeness.

There is a great amount of character to be noticed among the natives during a voyage on the lake, and although they are badly and even grotesquely dressed (for the pretty old costume has quite disappeared in this part of the country, and its modern substitute is hideous), still their old-fashioned manners and simple courtesy are very striking; and in spite of their love of a little mild ostentation they are so quiet and well behaved, that they would appear to great advantage if contrasted with the crowd that may be found say on a Greenwich steamer.

At Eidsvold we left the steamer for the train which was waiting to receive us, and about nightfall were once more in Christiania, and after a sumptuous supper went to rest in sumptuous beds, thinking ere we fell asleep of how to-morrow we should again have to submit ourselves to the yoke of civilisation, to discard our flannel shirts for linen ones and stick-up collars, to throw aside our shooting boots, and again bite off our nails, which have grown to their natural length under the soothing influence of a long spell of unworried conscience.

September 23.—We found Christiania this morning almost as hot as we left it, the streets all dry and dusty, and the trees parched for want of rain; and the sunshine was very pleasant as we wandered about the town into the various shops, purchasing articles by the assistance of which we hoped to attain popularity among our relatives on our arrival in England.

The shopkeepers were almost all very slow; in fact, the transaction of any business is not the hardy Norseman's strong point. We copy this extract from the Skipper's journal:—

'I went to the bank this morning to get some circular notes changed, and they kept me there fussing over them for fifty minutes before I got the money. During this time of expectation I read two letters from home through, and had a chase after a torpid fly on the floor with my stick: considering his languid condition this fly showed great spirit, but after following him about three feet along the floor and nine inches up the wall, I made a fortunate dash at him, and concluded his existence. Then I thought for a while and stared all round the room, and cut my nails with my knife. Then I counted how many boards there were in the floor, and how many nails there were on an average in each board, and made a little calculation on these figures to discover how many nails there were in the whole room, and what they weighed, how much they cost, how many miles they would reach if laid end to end, and how many men at how much an hour for how long it had taken to drive them all in. Then again I thought for a while, but still the money did not come, and my moral reflections on men and things had just led me to the conclusion that all mortals were but desolate creatures, and that I of all men was most desolate and abandoned, when at the end of forty minutes an official arrived with a sort of cheque. And after that it took ten minutes more to change the cheque into money in a lower room, where the clerks had their hair so beautifully brushed and were so haughty, that instead of being angry I could only thank them profusely for giving me the money at all.'

After finishing our hunt for curios, it occurred to us that we ought to see the viking's ship recently unearthed somewhere on the fjord, so we walked down to the University, where we were told by a student that it was not yet open to the public, but that if we would ask the Professor of Archæology, whom John profanely designated 'the boss that runs the antiquity show,' he had no doubt that, being strangers, we should be allowed to see the ship.

Would the fact of a man being a foreigner obtain his admission to a private view of an English curiosity, save perhaps the plans and mechanism of an ironclad or torpedo? Probably not.

Revolving these thoughts within our minds we sought the professor, and he at once left the work upon which he was engaged and took us to the ship, which was locked up inside a wooden building that has been erected for it.

Very interesting it was, the preservation of the wood and also the ironwork being wonderful. Unfortunately, some archæologists of earlier date than the present had also made some excavations in earch of memorials of the past. They had cut a large hole in the side amidships, for the purpose of carrying off the ornaments and other valuables by which the dead viking was surrounded, in the chamber constructed for his body right in the centre of the boat. The modern archæologists call their predecessors 'sacrilegious robbers,' but we are averse to the use of strong language among men of science.

However, the rest of the ship was perfect, even to the shields which used to adorn the gunwale, which are now seen to have been made of thin wood, and were probably only ornamental. She was a good big boat, rather flat-bottomed and low in the water, but with great breadth of beam, and built on lines that left no room for doubt as to her seagoing qualities.

The whole day was occupied by this shopping and sightseeing, and we went to bed more exhausted than by a hard day's stalking at Gjendin, and not half so much satisfied with our achievements.

It is almost unnecessary to mention that we found at the hotel a note from the Skipper, begging us to bring home a waterproof sheet and a few clothes that he had been obliged to leave there. We think that this young man must have shed nearly all his raiment before leaving Norway, and gone home clad in a yellow ulster which we know he had left at the hotel in July; for, judging from the fragments that we have picked up from time to time on our homeward route, he cannot have much other property with him except his gun, rifle, and fishing-gear.

CHAPTER XXXIV.

HOME AGAIN.

September 24.—To-day our Norwegian friends who lent us the hut at Rus Vand came to dine with us, and then saw us safely aboard the 'Angelo,' and at five o'clock, in the presence of an immense crowd which covered the whole quay, some of the people cheering, but many more weeping, we steamed out of the harbour.

As the sound of the last bell died away, and the last gangway fell with a crash on to the landing-stage, a hatless, breathless man rushed up the companion and darted at the spot where he supposed the gangway to be: seeing that he was too late, he yelled to the people on shore, and made as though he would have cast himself into the water, but was restrained by the passengers. Meanwhile a fleet of little boats endeavoured to catch a rope and be towed until he could be lowered into one of them; but all failed, and the unfortunate man was carried off to Christiansand, so that on his involuntary voyage he would have leisure to meditate on the folly of a too prolonged farewell.

With a gentle breeze we steamed down the fjord, which

never looked more lovely than on this evening; and so beautiful was the night, so warm, so radiant, and with such a depth of glorious colouring from the departed sun, that people crept away into the shade out of the *moonlight*, from pure force of habit, after the heat of the summer.

The influence of such a night, together with a certain sense of something completed; the calm ocean all round us, and the soothing, monotonous throbbing of the untiring screw, produced a longing for confidence in John's bosom, so that he gave utterance to his sentiments as he leant with Esau over the rail of the hurricane deck, and watched the ever-sparkling phosphorescent lights caused by the passage of the vessel through the quiet water.

'Yes, I'm sorry to be leaving Norway, for, you know, there's something delightful to me about the simplicity of the people' (Esau's mind reverted to Ivar Tofte and his plate cupboard); 'they seem to place a childlike confidence in a stranger, which is quite incomprehensible to me. Then there is an unwordable calm, an indescribable tranquillity, which seems to cling both to the country and its inhabitants; even the houses seem to possess an imperturbable serenity of demeanour which you will not find on any other island in Europe. In fact, y'know, Esau, it's a country where one might live quietly and die in peace, where "moths do not corrupt, neither do worms break through and steal," don't you know, Esau? And I'm deuced sorry to have to count among past memories the time we have spent here, where the unbroken harmony of existence is that repose for which my soul has longed these many years; but never until now, no, by George! never, has it been able to discover the most uncertain tracings of its ideal.'

Here Esau, who had his deck shoes on, seeing what sort of a mood John was in, stole away quietly towards the cabin, and left him prosing on to the German Ocean. He paused, however, a moment before descending the companion stairs, and caught a few more words which, as the moon had now set, John was confiding to the darkness.

'A couple more days, and we shall be back in England, where, y'know, I think civilisation is overdone. My existence there is a perpetual state of toadying and being toadied: you see, it's a place where the serpent of social emulation creeps into our very beds, and hangs suspended over our heads by a mere thread when we least expect him; and, y'know, Esau' — But Esau had slunk down the stairs, and the rest of this impassioned outburst is, we fear, lost to humanity.

September 25.—We woke up to find ourselves just leaving Christiansand, and soon reached the lighthouse at what the Skipper calls 'the bottom left-hand corner of Norway,' but remained in bed while we glared at it through the port.

We were taking out a great number of emigrants for America, fine, sturdy-looking young fellows, probably as hard as nails, and quite equal to coping with the difficulties of a new country. They all looked so cheery and full of hope and expectation, that we could not help thinking rather sadly of the day when they will wake up to some of the unpleasant realities of Yankee life, and wish themselves back again in their native hills among their own simple-minded friends.

The day passed in the manner usual at sea when the water is smooth and the ship goes merrily homeward bound. Hardly any one missed a meal—rather a difference from the ordinary state of affairs in the wild North Sea; and at evening the sun went down in a blaze of scarlet and gold, which was reflected from the perfectly calm surface; and we turned in with tranquil minds, even Esau being now reasonably hopeful of seeing the Humber without suffering the pangs of starvation.

Esau is not a good sailor. On the last occasion of our return from Norway he crossed by the 'Angelo' a fortnight before the Skipper; and the latter, on arriving on board prepared for the voyage, saw the steward, and asked him, 'What sort of a passage did you have last trip, George?'

'Beautiful, sir. I never see a smoother sea.'

Then the Skipper went on, 'Did you see anything of Mr. Esau on the voyage?'

To which George replied, 'I seen him come aboard.'

And this brief remark of George's conveyed a world of untold fact.

September 26.—We dropped anchor outside Hull at half-past five this evening, in the remainder of the very same drizzling rain that was going on when we left England in July. Hull on Sunday in a soaking rain is not a place to grow romantic about, so we omit all reference to our first sensations and maledictions on our return to our native climate, and proceed to a more agreeable subject—dinner.

It was a merry meal in company with four of our fellow passengers, who were likewise returning from sport in Norway—two from salmon fishing, two from red-deer stalking, and with whom there was consequently a bond of sympathy.

With these kindred spirits, after British beef had been washed down with British beer, a Skaal drunk in British champagne, and tongues were loosened by the confidential pipe and British cigar, we chatted long and pleasantly; wandering again with rod and gun among the rugged mountains of that wild north land, recalling exploits performed, and perhaps indulging in those mild and harmless exaggerations of doughty deeds which no traveller or sportsman can resist. Already we found ourselves forgetting the few disagreeable incidents that occurred during our trip, and viewing everything through that rosy mist which happily arises before all past hours of pleasure and discomfort alike. Too soon bed-time put an end to our retrospect, and we slept the sleep of the wearied traveller, with dreams of trout, ryper, and rein-deer—steamboat, cariole, and sleigh—mountain, lake, and river—tent and sæter—paddle and pony—hurrying through our brains in wild confusion.

To-morrow, alas! we commence again a life of gilded misery and gloomy magnificence. Give to us the untrammelled freedom of 'Gammle Norge,' and the humble crust of flad-brod—*with* JAM.